The Beating
of
My Hearts

The Beating
of
My Hearts

A Tale Of Two Hearts:
Their disease, their treatment, and their cure

Brian L. Fowler, MD

WESTBOW
PRESS
A DIVISION OF THOMAS NELSON

NIV – New International Version
Scriptures taken from the Holy Bible, New International Version®, NIV®. Copyright ©
1973, 1978, 1984, 2011 by Biblica, Inc.™ Used by permission of Zondervan. All rights
reserved worldwide. www.zondervan.com The "NIV" and "New International Version" are
trademarks registered in the United States Patent and Trademark Office by Biblica, Inc.™
Scripture taken from the Good News Translation - Second Edition,
Copyright 1992 by American Bible Society. Used by Permission.
Used by permission Excerpts taken from What Every Christian Ought
to Know by Adrian Rogers c 2007 B&H Publishing Group.
The Middle
Words and Music by Bebo Norman Copyright © 2010 New Spring Publishing (ASCAP)
/ Appstreet Music (ASCAP). All rights for the world on behalf of Appstreet Music
administered by New Spring Publishing. All Rights Reserved. Used By Permission.
Fix You
Words and Music by Guy Berryman, Jon Buckland, Will Champion and Chris
Martin Copyright © 2005 by Universal Music Publishing MGB Ltd. All Rights in the
United States Administered by Universal Music - MGB Songs International Copyright
Secured All Rights Reserved Reprinted by Permission of Hal Leonard Corporation.

Book cover design by Alan Belcher, Rudkin Productions LLC.

WestBow Press books may be ordered through booksellers or by contacting:
WestBow Press
A Division of Thomas Nelson
1663 Liberty Drive
Bloomington, IN 47403
www.westbowpress.com
1-(866) 928-1240

Certain stock imagery © Thinkstock.
ISBN: 978-1-4497-8422-5 (sc)
ISBN: 978-1-4497-8424-9 (hc)
ISBN: 978-1-4497-8423-2 (e)
Library of Congress Control Number: 2013902285
Printed in the United States of America
WestBow Press rev. date: 5/13/2013

Contents

The Prelude

The Conversation

I. Preparing My Heart

The Conversation

II. Cardioversion

III. Recovery

IV. A New View

V. True Healing

A heartbeat generates a palpable pulse approximately ninety thousand times every day. Too many beats missed, the mind becomes confused, the body collapses, and life ends.

The spiritual heart beats forever.

To God be the Glory

Search me, O God, and know my heart;
test me and know my anxious thoughts.
See if there is any offensive way in me,
and lead me in the way everlasting.

—Psalm 139:23–24

Acknowledgments

I am fortunate and blessed to be married to my wife, Cindy, who has been the love of my life for twenty-seven years. Our love for each other continues to grow with each trial faced. Her encouragement has helped me write this book. I have appreciated the numerous discussions along the way.

Morgen and Wil were courageous and supportive. Their love carried me through many tough times.

My staff and colleagues at the Urgent Care & Occupational Health Centers of Texas, PA are the best coworkers and doctors around. Physicians, your selfless willingness to step in and work the extra shifts while I was out of commission is forever appreciated and will take a lifetime to repay.

To the cardiologists, pulmonologists, rheumatologist, and your staffs in Cleveland and San Antonio; the tireless day and night shift nurses who cared for me during my hospitalizations; the Medtronic techs; and all the healthcare professionals who were instrumental in my care, I can only say, thank you. Your commitment to your profession is admirable and will always be treasured by this very appreciative patient.

Finally, I want to thank God for every one of you. My hope is that each of you will be touched by my (our) story and that the peace of God will comfort you always.

Introduction

I thought I knew what being a patient was all about, especially after treating more than one hundred thousand as an emergency medicine and urgent care physician over the last twenty-three years. But I hadn't a clue.

Patients present to emergency rooms (ERs) with illnesses as simple as the common cold and as devastating as a rupturing abdominal aortic aneurysm. The varied illnesses often present simultaneously without warning and commonly get placed in adjoining rooms by unsuspecting staff. Their unexpected suddenness in presentation requires an ER staff to maintain a keen alertness that's often difficult to sustain at four o'clock in the morning after a grueling night shift. The contrast in their management and treatment is extreme.

The emergency room with its whirlwind twenty-four-hour-a-day pace continuously filled with sick and dying patients and stressed family members creates the perfect medium for a social worker's nightmare and can cause a roller coaster of emotions for the health care worker. Personally, I often would protect myself from such fluctuations in emotion by detaching my mind and spirit from the patient's grave circumstances. This protective suit of armor was manifested by a monotone, colorless, bland persona and mind-set. My stoic approach protected me, the caregiver, from getting too involved emotionally, but unfortunately, it also created a vacuum between my perception and what the patient was actually suffering. This mental state, I thought, would allow me to perform at my very best during what most would consider a very difficult situation. I didn't see the opportunities lost and insights not gained because of my approach.

Today, I'm a better physician because of what I've endured and learned as a patient these past couple of years, but more importantly, I am a better man because of what has been illustrated and revealed to me during times of fear and doubt. I am more assured in my relationship with God now, and I better understand His desire for my presence. In no way do I feel I have "earned my wings" by some great act I have accomplished for God, but actually quite the opposite. I have developed a renewed understanding of God and who He really is, why He loves me, and why He desires my attention daily. My renewed mind and spirit have allowed me to better understand that I have done *nothing* to earn this love and forgiveness, and I can't do anything to lose it either.

I have eagerly pursued God since being diagnosed with not one but two insidious heart diseases. Struggling with their symptoms and complications created an opportunity for "my clay" to become malleable and receptive to God's firm yet gentle touch. I use the term *clay* because I like the analogy comparing Christian life to the potter, his wheel, and the clay. The clay represents me and includes my God-given faith, thoughts, feelings, and expressions. Its consistency embodies my willingness to be molded. The potter doesn't mold without the clay spinning, so the revolving wheel upon which the clay rests symbolizes the trials, hardships, and victories that create motion in my life. When the potter's hand is pressed against my non-sedentary clay, He creates the changes He desires *in* me. The potter, of course, is God. One notable contrast in this analogy relates to the potter's technique, for the earthly potter molds from the outside in, while the Master Potter molds from the *inside out.*

During my journey, God magically reshaped a new heart at the center of my "clay," and from it overflows an outward expression of the spirit that has been poured into its chambers. His technique of molding seemed painstakingly slow at times, and yet at other moments, the wheel appeared to be spinning out of control. However, the Potter remained steadfast while constantly applying the perfect amount of pressure for the precise amount of time. His gentle touch yielded intricate facets in my clay like love, joy, peace, patience, kindness, goodness, faithfulness, gentleness and self-control (Galatians 5:22–23). My life and who I am in Christ represents a beautiful vessel being molded by the Potter since becoming a Christian thirty-six years ago. My vessel's characteristics are refined often, and I appreciate and accept the changes He sculpts during my trials and suffering. I know He ceaselessly creates what is pleasing to Him.

Between June, 2009, and December, 2011, my "wheel" (life) began rotating rapidly and was filled with multiple visits to hospitals, doctors' offices, labs, and imaging centers—the usual places one becomes all too familiar with when a serious illness threatens. The coldness of the hospital rooms with their sharps containers hanging on the walls, rigid exam tables with the crinkly paper, claustrophobic MRI machines and PET scanners, and the never-ending, incessant beeping of IV monitors throughout the night made for an uncomfortable environment for a patient who desired more comfort than any other time in his life. Unfortunately, it seems that while being healed a patient has to learn to live with these annoyances because it is part of the treatment process. Patients trust their physicians to provide therapies that will improve their outcomes while often never knowing the therapy may make their bodies worse before getting better. The patient endures until the bitter end, never losing hope of a cure, or at least a portion of one. This hope allows him or her to strive for a few additional invaluable moments that can be shared with family, friends, and loved ones. During this treatment process, almost any type of therapy is permitted in order to avoid that ever-present potential final outcome we all know as death. My perception of this "threat" has immensely changed since beginning my journey. My associated fear is being whittled away.

Each of us has stories related to our struggles and their associated defeats or triumphs. If you are facing such a challenge and it's leading you to question your faith or doubt your relationship with God, I hope my story will provide you encouragement and be a reminder that *nothing* can separate you from the love of God.

The Prelude

Chapter 1

The Trials of Life

"It isn't your actions, but your reactions," my dad taught, "that illustrate the type of mettle of which you are truly made." Meaning that my character, of course, would be revealed by the way "I weathered the storm."

My identity has been shaken recently after discovering that my reaction to the greatest catastrophe of my life was an inordinate fear of death. A fear cultivated by doubt in my relationship with God, which resulted in confusion about whether I would be accepted into heaven for eternity. I was questioning basic truths known by the average Christian as expressed in the verses John 10:28, Philippians 1:6, and Romans 4:7. For some reason, my confidence in these truths had dissipated and caused me to question my relationship with Christ. I thought I believed in Christ, but I wasn't sure my life illustrated enough change, enough running from sin and not to it, and enough service, which I knew was not required for salvation but nonetheless represented my relationship, or lack thereof, with God. After all, what did my life represent? Did I live for Christ or for me? I knew what the answer was supposed to be, but when faced with a reflection of my past, the answer appeared quite unattractive. Like everyone, I have had certain events in the past where I wish I had responded differently. My reaction or response to each event illustrated my orientation to the world and my relationship with God at the time.

My responses to previous trials set me up for years of drought and famine in my Christian life. I lived in the spring well of mercy and grace, yet like the Jews with Moses, I too didn't appreciate the manna and water provided daily. I know God starts a good work in each of us and carries it to completion (again Philippians 1:6), but I had lost sight of His presence. My eyes were closed. I began to doubt if He was still interested in me, never realizing it was I who was losing interest in Him.

Today, as I begin writing these pages, I am sitting in my eighty-six-year-old, demented father's hospital room, waiting on his blood transfusion (third time in five months) to treat his severe anemia, which is secondary to a myeloproliferative disorder (bone marrow/pre-leukemic condition). He looked into my eyes with sincerity through his mental haze and asked, "How many times do you think they will do this?" I smiled and responded, "As many times as they need, I guess." I could tell he was thinking about how many times *he* wanted to do it, but our discussion didn't go there today.

Life is full of decisions related to the trials or tests I'm presented. How I respond to these trials is what makes all the difference and illustrates my inner core or belief system. My recent trial knocked me to my knees, literally. In 2009, I began a sojourn through a dry and isolated desert. It has become the greatest journey I have ever traveled. How I "weathered this storm" has made all the difference, and the make of my true mettle has been revealed.

Chapter 2

I Love My Life!

I live in a quaint town of German heritage named Boerne with a population of about ten thousand situated deep in the Texas Hill Country. It's the place my wife, Cindy, and I settled after we left the navy with our two children, Morgen and Wil. We were married in Boerne in 1985 while we were students in nearby San Antonio. I was in medical school at the University of Texas Health Science Center at San Antonio, and Cindy attended Our Lady of the Lake University's Worden School of Social Work. We recited our vows in the beautiful stone chapel of Saint Helena's Episcopal Church located in the center of town on Main Street. Returning to Boerne felt like coming home.

Saint Helena's Episcopal Church.

We live in a picturesque Victorian home built in 1907 on a street named after the state tree of Texas, Pecan Street. It's the place you hope to find at the end of your search for the perfect bed-and-breakfast. It is filled with all the luxuries and amenities I could ever want. The house is a half block off Main Street, and in the mornings, I can hear church bells ringing from either the Lutheran or Catholic churches a few blocks away.

Our Home on Pecan Street.

There's a bakery called Bear Moon that my friends, Paula and Jack, own just around the corner. In the mornings the bakery's large exhaust fans fill the downtown air with heavenly aromas that tempt the soul. When the wind is from the northwest, the tantalizing fragrance drifts toward our home. Its lure is overwhelming and cannot be denied.

Bear Moon Bakery on Main Street in Boerne

Later in the day, the smell of Texas barbecue fills our olfactories from the Shell gas station/barbecue restaurant/grocery store called the Riverside Market behind our house. Two blocks over is a microbrewery, The Dodging Duck, owned by Keith and his wife, Chandra. Keith used to play trumpet in the University of Texas Longhorn Band. Their microbrewery/restaurant sits on a beautiful picturesque waterway called the Cibolo Creek, whose stream flows through the center of town. Every summer, we watch Fourth of July fireworks reflect off its mirror-like surface.

The Cibolo Creek just down the street from our house.

The creek is always filled with geese, ducks, egrets, and sunbathing turtles. I love that each of these sensory stimuli are within viewing, hearing, and smelling distance of my front yard. I guess you could say I like living here.

I'm thankful for the opportunities I've been given while living in Boerne. Cindy and I helped establish a school in 1999 named The Geneva School of Boerne with two other couples, the Wackers and the Thorntons. Geneva is a classical/Christian private school, which initially enrolled thirteen students and now enrolls 580 students with a waiting list. Our daughter Morgen was a member of the 2011 graduating class, which happened to be the first class to walk across the commencement stage and receive a coveted Geneva diploma.

The Geneva School of Boerne

I no longer commute to San Antonio hospitals, for I have left the stressful life of the emergency room where I had worked as an emergency physician for greater than twenty years. I now work less than a quarter mile from my house at the Urgent Care & Occupational Health Centers of Texas clinic that I opened seven years ago with a colleague from the ER, Dr. Bryan Dunn.

In 2009, I knew I was blessed and looked forward to enjoying life to its fullest. After all, I was only fifty years of age and in great health. I had worked diligently throughout my life, and it finally seemed to be paying off.

Chapter 3

How Did I Get Here?

While it seemed my life was heading in the right direction in 2009, I knew there was one facet that needed some special attention. I had so many holes in a lacework of prayer, church attendance, Bible study, and service. Yes, when looking at my spiritual life, one saw a wedge of Swiss cheese. When a bite was taken, it was mostly air and very little cheese. Where was the density in my Christian life? Perhaps a brief history of my spiritual development is needed.

By the age of sixteen, my exposure to religion consisted primarily of my older brother, sister, and I going to church on Easter with my mom. We would sit in a pew feeling awkward while wearing our new Easter outfits beside people we had never met in a building we had never gone. Easter, you see, was the only Sunday we ever went to church.

My dad on Sunday mornings wore his "wife-beater" T-shirt while watering the yard. He would spot Jehovah Witnesses (JWs) coming up the street and engage them in conversation about their religion while sitting on his ribbon-laced lawn chair with the ripped seat. He would wait until the perfect moment and then ask, "Do you ever salute the flag?" knowing their religion didn't approve of this act. He would animatedly share how he had spent twenty years in the navy defending the rights of Americans in order that folks like them could freely worship as they pleased. He also would reiterate how important it was to serve your country. I was embarrassed for them. My dad loved each opportunity to express his form of religion. After awhile, even the JWs stopped coming by.

My faith and spiritual conviction to follow Christ were first evident when, at the age of seventeen, I gave my life to Christ at a youth conference in Fort Worth, Texas. I had been going to a few Wednesday night youth meetings sponsored by the Baptist Church in my hometown. The youth meetings were called "Sonny and Share." Can you believe that name?

I was invited to attend by friends I had known since first grade. I always liked this group of kids, and I knew what made them different. They always meant well when speaking about Christ to me, but I wasn't willing to give up my life to Him just yet. I had far too many enjoyable things I still needed to accomplish as a sixteen-year-old Texan, and I wasn't ready to give that up for nobody, no how! I wasn't going to let the stringent Christian lifestyle from a small Texas town where beer and liquor couldn't be served keep me from living life to its fullest. I thought the restrictions of the church in my Bible-Belt world were stifling and kept a young man from enjoying life. *After all, I'm a good guy and am friends with everyone*, I thought. *What do I need church for any way?* I knew what I needed, and it wasn't a Savior. All I needed was a friend who would drink a few beers with me on a Friday night while riding around in my vinyl-roofed Malibu with the hope of picking up a couple of girls. If God wanted to take that away from me, He would have to wait. My shallowness was typical of many teenagers from my small town at the time. I wasn't any different from the rest.

Later that summer, between my junior and senior years of high school, I was invited to a special youth event sponsored by the same Baptist Church called "Underground Church." It was another youth meeting, and it tried to recreate living in a country where going to a Christian gathering was illegal. It was exciting and allowed me to hear for the first time the gospel of Jesus Christ like I had never heard before.

The first night of Underground Church, I stood with trepidation next to my friends as we gathered on the bank of our town lake at a predetermined rendezvous site around dusk as instructed by a secret communiqué. We waited a few minutes, and then boats with spotlights started to approach, one by one. Everyone was whispering, and I thought, *Boy, these guys are really taking this stuff seriously.* The boats took us to an island where earlier in the day the men of the Baptist Church had mowed, prepared a campfire, and set up logs to sit on. The youth minister, Mike, shared some funny stories and then a message about Christ, why He came and what He meant to this world. His words took me by surprise. *Becoming a Christian seems so simple*, I thought. *Almost too simple.* I was used to earning my way into organizations and clubs. If *anyone* could be a member, why would I want to join such a club? What did being a member really represent? What would it provide *me*? Understanding what was being offered that night didn't sink in for a while, but it did plant a seed. After the meeting, I continued with my life that I loved so dearly.

The last meeting of Underground Church occurred in the basement of an old church near the east side of town. The church had primarily a black congregation and was located in a part of town most white kids didn't venture into at night or pretty much during the day. Being there made each participant feel like they didn't belong, which was exactly the setting the youth pastor hoped to create. While he shared his message in the dank basement, a sudden chaos consumed the room as local police raided the gathering and took the entire group to jail. *WOW!* I thought. *What a great plan!* I missed that meeting, but I didn't need to be there, for the Holy Spirit was already working on me since I left the previous meeting at the lake. While driving home, I thought about what I had heard about Christ, His life, and His teachings. A strange sensation came over me, and I thought, *Someone's in my backseat.* I turned around slowly and checked to make sure the seat was empty. It was.

My greater understanding of why Christ came to this earth as explained by His sacrifice and witnessed resurrection, which resulted in forgiveness for all who believe, coupled with the Holy Spirit's conviction of my heart related to sin in my life triggered thoughts and questions my skeptical mind had never considered. Questions like "Why do I exist?" and "For what purpose?" to "Who is Christ?" and "What is His significance to me?" consumed my thinking. Their depth extended to the abyss of my hardened heart. The cumulative effect of my thinking reached a climax later that summer at a Christian youth rally on the TCU campus in Fort Worth.

I attended the rally with about a dozen friends from my town. We listened to various speakers throughout the day, but the last one concluded his talk with a unique invitation. He invited anyone who didn't know Christ yet wanted to have a personal relationship with Him to pray with him and to ask Jesus into his or her heart as Lord and Savior. I had witnessed a similar request as a kid while watching the Billy Graham crusade with my family on our black-and-white television. People attending the crusade responded to Reverend Graham's invitation by leaving their seats, walking down to the stadium or arena floor, and then congregating around his podium. With tears streaming down their cheeks, I could tell even as a ten year old that those responding were dealing with significant issues in their lives, and that their decisions perhaps were life changing. My juvenile yet inquisitive mind became intrigued by the unusual event unfolding in the middle of my family's living room while being broadcast to a national audience, but I never inquired of my parents or older siblings about the meaning of what was happening. In our home, such things were never discussed. I would have to wait a few years to get my answer.

In Fort Worth, seven years after viewing the Billy Graham crusade on television, I was witnessing a similar request by the speaker who was standing on the elevated stage atop the arena floor, but this time, I was the one in the stands being asked to stand up, walk down the steps to admit I was a sinner incapable of living a sinless life, and acknowledge Christ as God's Son who died on a cross in order to be the lone sacrifice once and for all for the sins of the world. Responding would start the process of living a new life with God and as His adopted son. I would be acknowledging that all of my sins were forgiven and I had been given eternal life.

I observed others walking down the steps leading to the stage on the arena's floor. I wanted to join them, but such turmoil existed in my mind. I stood there with significant unease and looked forward to the awkward moment being over. I began to reflect on the words I had heard that summer about Christ and the lives of friends who had accepted Him. I thought about Christ's life and sacrifice and what it meant to the world and to me.

A wrestling match commenced in my heart between God and an opposing foe. While standing there, it finally made sense to me who His opponent was. It was me; all my selfishness, loneliness, and desire to seek something out there but never knowing what I was looking for. Who I was and understood myself to be without God was poignantly revealed at this critical moment. "It's not about me," I quietly acknowledged. I knew there was something more, and it made sense for the first time in my life.

The invitation music was still playing as I stepped out into the aisle and made the long walk down the stadium stairs. Tears were now streaming down my face as I proclaimed, "It's yours God. You have all of me." I gave my life to Christ that day, and the freedom I felt when God lifted my burden of sin was humbling and wonderful. I knew I had changed forever.

I drove home, wondering what I would tell my parents about my decision. When I got home, I just told them the truth, "I accepted Christ as my Savior today."

My parents knew *of* Christ, but I wasn't sure if they really *knew* Him. Both were raised in Christian homes. My mother was the daughter of Dutch immigrants who went to a Dutch Reform Church in Sioux Center, Iowa. Her family went twice on Sundays, and all sermons were spoken in Dutch, which she never understood. My father attended church every Sunday in a small, wooden Methodist Church in Friendship, Texas, that held about thirty people. It was near his father's one-hundred-acre cotton farm, which produced one bale of cotton annually if the rain came. Going to church was usually the only social event he ever got to participate in during the week. When I became a Christian, I don't think either of my parents had developed a personal relationship with God through Christ and the Holy Spirit. At least, they hadn't shared it with me. The desire of their hearts was vague and unknown to me.

After becoming a Christian, my partying, drinking, etc. was curtailed. I started being "discipled" by the part-time youth pastor at the Baptist Church who I had met at Underground Church. He guided me through the basic tenants of the Christian faith, and we had the opportunity to witness to some of my fellow classmates at my high school. I was definitely on fire for Jesus. Senior year came and ended. I left for college, leaving my home of eighteen years.

Since those early years after accepting Christ as my Savior, I have continued my faith journey but with limited discipline, which has lead to anemic Christian growth and maturity. In 2009, I was regularly attending Sunday services with my family. I had gone to various retreats throughout the previous years, which usually provided a temporary Christian "high." I mentioned I helped start a classical/Christian school in our town in 1999, but after serving on its board for six years, I gradually vacated my relationship and usually only went back for my children's functions. Over the years, I hadn't forgotten what I believed, but I hadn't done much either to illustrate that belief, which resulted in a mind-set of compromise and lack of assurance. I never seemed to have that "spark" I saw in so many others at church and in the school who were turned on for Jesus. Why wasn't I more engaged? What held me back from being more like them? The answers were always there, but I wasn't interested in finding them.

In 2009, a new chapter was being written related to my spiritual life, but I didn't know the page was turning. It started on a warm June morning, coinciding with a change in the beating of my "hearts."

Chapter 4

Two Titanics

On a beautiful June morning in 2009, I had just completed my jog through downtown Boerne. I had run past Saint Helena's Episcopal Church where Cindy and I were married. From there, I could smell Bear Moon Bakery all the way down Main Street. After my run, I sat next to the pool, cooling off with a glass of ice-cold water. As I sat, I noticed my heart rate remained 110–120 bpm (beats per minute), and it lasted for fifteen minutes. *That's odd*, I thought, but I figured I was dehydrated, as it was unusually warm that day. My heart rate eventually returned to normal, and no further episodes occurred the rest of the day. Later that week, and again after running, a similar event occurred that piqued my attention greatly, so I decided to visit a cardiologist. After all, I was going to turn fifty the following month, so it wouldn't hurt to get a baseline of my heart's status.

Now, I would never say doctors make great patients, but I was willing to step into the role and make the best of it. I had never been plagued with a major medical condition in the past, and I wasn't expecting anything major right now. But after working in emergency rooms for years and having witnessed patients with mild yet cunning symptoms that present like tips of icebergs, I knew to be cautious and prepared for anything. Some icebergs are ferociously huge and easily hidden under and disguised by quiet seas and can lead to horrible disasters like the Titanic.

In *Tales of a Wayside Inn*, "The Theologian's Tale," a poem by Henry Wadsworth Longfellow (1863), he speaks of "Ships that pass in the night." Well, my life was about to have *two* Titanics pass one another, but unlike Longfellow's two ships that "speak (to) each other in passing, only a signal shown, and a distant voice in (the) darkness," mine were on a collision course headed for the same iceberg. Each of my Titanics represented a heart: one physical and the other spiritual. In the summer of 2009, both were navigating through treacherous waters, for the "iceberg" they were careening toward drifted ominously ahead.

After visiting with my cardiologist, I underwent a nuclear stress test, echocardiogram, EKG, and a twenty-four-hour Holter monitor. As expected, all tests were completely normal. "See, I *don't* have a heart problem," I noted with a sigh of relief. Disaster averted, and life got to keep moving forward at the brisk pace I was accustomed. My heart was fine, and the heart specialist had proven it.

Because of the type of symptoms I was presenting, my cardiologist questioned me about another "iceberg" that might be floating around in my "unchartered waters" kindly known as *stress*. I certainly had many things going on in my life, and perhaps it was having an impact on my body. I agreed this might be an issue, for after all, I was almost fifty years old and in the "sandwich generation" where we take care of kids on one side and aging parents on the other. I had recently moved my parents into an assisted living center in Boerne and was co-owner of two successful Urgent Care clinics that saw approximately thirty thousand patients a year and was planning a third clinic. I had two teenaged children, and one was applying to college. Maybe it was time to reassess my life and see what I could do to reduce stress and calm my heart down. If I started taking it easy, eating better, and lost a few pounds, I would be healthier than ever. *Life is still good*, I thought after being assured I had nothing to worry about. All that was required of me was a slight change in my "ship's" course. No major redirection required.

At the time, I must admit, I wondered if there was more than one "iceberg" floating nearby in the icy waters I was navigating. I hoped not, for I knew the "hulls" of my "ships" (hearts) were vulnerable due to their weakened states caused by years of neglect and lack of maintenance. If impacted, the consequences could be significant and life changing.

Chapter 5

Improbable Firsts

My life for whatever reason has been filled with improbable firsts, or first-time experiences associated with a very low statistical chance of happening. The decisions I made in response to these events affected me greatly and caused significant wear and tear on my relationship with Christ. My responses were often calculated yet at other times were just a reflex, as they were not conditioned to respond in a Christ-like manner during chaotic times, for my faith was immature.

Of these firsts, I will share only a few to illustrate their impact on the *spiritual* Titanic that was sailing aimlessly through my treacherous, "shadow of death" seas. These events were not planned, and I would have never predicted their occurrence. Regardless of their improbability, though, they were still used by God to influence my path. In retrospect, I can see His hand lifting me up each time I stumbled. "If the Lord delights in a man's way, He makes his steps firm; though he stumble, he will not fall, for the LORD upholds him with His hand" (Psalm 37:23–24).

One of the "Firsts"

I had applied for and received a Navy Health Professions scholarship to attend medical school, and after medical school, I owed the navy eight years of service as a physician. I had just completed my internship (first year of medical training) in obstetrics and gynecology, or OB-GYN, at the Balboa Naval Hospital in San Diego, California. Soon afterward, I was assigned to be the medical officer of Destroyer Squadron Seven (ComDesRon7). I will forever treasure my memories related to serving as a staff member of this unit, but I would like to share one in particular from my very first navy cruise.

My inaugural navy voyage took me up the coastline of California. I had never been at sea before, and the only event that even came close was a "booze cruise" from Puerto Vallarta to Yelapa Island aboard a small charter boat in which I spent the entire trip puking my brains out from the severe sea sickness I developed within five minutes of leaving the dock. I wasn't sure how I would react to the seas aboard a much larger navy vessel, but I was willing to give it a try. Actually, I didn't have much of a choice.

I was a member of the crew of a Spruance-class destroyer known as the USS *John Young*. We were accompanied by another ship, a frigate called the USS Schofield, and were steaming up the coast together, heading north to rejoin the remaining ships of our battle group in Vancouver, British Columbia.

On a late afternoon just north of San Francisco, my ship received a disturbing radio call from a distressed Filipino Independent Duty Corpsman (IDC) aboard the Schofield. I took the call in a dark, red-lit room known as the combat information center, or CIC, which increased the drama and intensity of each pressured word the IDC spoke. He had a very strong accent, making the transmitted information difficult to understand, especially since our poor connection was over a secured two-way satellite radio. It sounded like his patient was having a severe asthma attack.

Asthmatics aren't allowed to enlist in the navy because of this very situation, I thought to myself as I was figuring out what to do. I doubted my IDC's diagnosis initially, but as I listened to the labored breathing of his patient in the background noise on the radio, I soon concluded that my corpsman was correct. At that moment, I could have strangled the navy recruiter's neck who had signed this kid up for duty, but I had work to do, and there was nothing I could do about it right then. After informing the captain of the USS John Young that I needed to transfer a special piece of medical equipment to the other ship, he prepared to navigate the USS *John Young* so it would be positioned alongside the Schofield. He performed the maneuver, known as an UNREP, with the finesse of an Indy 500 racecar driver pulling into a pit stop. I couldn't believe how well this guy guided his eight-thousand-ton ship. I had heard of the UNREP, which stands for "underway replenishment," maneuver in my physician sea school, and it requires an exceptionally skilled crew, as it is a method of transferring fuel, munitions, and stores from one ship to another while underway. A sharpshooting seaman uses a shotgun to fire a rope line to the other ship. The rope is then used to begin the process of exchanging lines, back and forth, until a strong cable is finally strewn between the ships. This occurs while the ships cruise parallel to one another in rough seas at twelve to sixteen knots.

Once the USS *John Young* and USS *Schofield* were tethered, I sent a nebulizer (aerosolizing device for administering asthma medications) with some additional medications to the Schofield via the cable. Since asthmatics were not allowed in the Navy, many of the smaller ships never carried this type of equipment. The only reason I had it with me was because we were going to take on civilians (known as Tigers) for a "Tiger Cruise" during our trip back to San Diego from Vancouver, and one of the civilian "Tigers" had a history of asthma.

We remained connected to the Schofield with the captains of the two ships maintaining a parallel course while sustaining a thirty- to forty-meter spread between ships. Seas were rough, as they are often known to be north of San Francisco. Additional treatments with the nebulizer and an IV steroid (Solumedrol) didn't improve the sailor's condition, and I knew my options for therapy were strained. Knowing this, the USS *John Young*'s captain asked with a wry grin, "Doc, do you want to be sent over to the Schofield by a chair attached to the cable?" I was already feeling queasy from seasickness but now a much greater sickening sensation developed from the thought of being hoisted and shimmied across a cable over the churning Pacific.

As I stood on the bridge with all eyes of the crew affixed upon my pale face, I remembered the last words I had heard from a sage, Jack Palance-type instructor at the Sea School for Doctors course I had attended in San Diego a few weeks prior. In a deep, gravelly voice while slowly exhaling cigarette smoke through his teeth, he warned, "Never ever let them place you in that damn chair between ships. There are *plenty* of sailors, but only *one* doctor!"

I had many times been soaked by a gush of amniotic fluid during deliveries the previous year while training in OB-GYN, but in no way was I prepared to be splashed in the cold Pacific hanging on a cable between two ships at dusk while sitting in a precariously suspended chair! The instructor's words were echoing in my head as I listened to the smiling captain asking me what I wanted to do for the sick sailor. I thought quickly and then asked the Captain, "Is there any helicopter support nearby, as we have no helicopters on either ship? The patient sounds pretty sick, and the IDC's voice is getting higher pitched each time he radios with the status of his patient." I explained to the captain that I probably needed to get this guy off the ship and to a hospital since we weren't going to be in Vancouver for two and half more days. Here I was with my OB-GYN internship training, surrounded by five hundred-plus men and an asthmatic that sounded like he was getting worse by the minute who wasn't even supposed to be in the navy. I couldn't believe my luck and all on my first navy cruise. What were the chances?

I convinced the captain and myself that I really needed to get the USS *Schofield* patient off the ship immediately. I couldn't admit my absolute fear, no, terror, of riding that chair over to the other ship to the captain, but I'm sure he read it in my eyes quite easily.

I don't know if I prayed for a helicopter that day, but whether I did or not, we got one from the Coast Guard out of Coos Bay, Oregon. I jumped aboard the helicopter when it finally arrived, and we went to the other ship. The flight crew had to hoist the patient in a litter since the helicopter couldn't land on the frigate's deck. I got the patient admitted to Coos Bay General Hospital and turned his care over to a local pulmonologist (lung doctor). I was later told that the sailor nearly got intubated (placed on a ventilator) that night.

It's funny how God works in our lives. He just keeps participating, no matter how far we wander off, in order to guide and encourage us back to a path that leads to Him. He continues working in our lives even though we are clueless of His presence. God knew my thoughts and fears aboard the USS *John Young* that day, and I wish I could say I had gone to Him and sought His guidance when I felt so stressed. But I didn't. My thoughts were far away from His teachings at that time in my life. He would continue, however, to never let me go. He remained ever vigilant, reminding me throughout the years of His love and forgiveness.

Chapter 6

What Did You Say?

Of my "firsts," there are three in particular that confused me greatly and later caused me to develop significant wrong thinking relative to my Christian faith. They affected me harshly and caused me to turn my back on God when I needed Him most, resulting in a lukewarm Christian life that lasted many years. These three "firsts" and my reaction to them yielded years of consequences and suffering.

The first of these began while I was in college. A friend introduced me to a cute, tall co-ed with long, blonde hair pulled back in a ponytail. I discovered she had grown up near my hometown, yet I had never seen her before. We talked for a few minutes, but I had studying to do, for it was near finals week, so I said, "Nice to meet you" and took off for the library. Finals week came and went, and I returned home for the summer.

While working that summer, I attended a couple of classes at the local junior college. I went to class wearing my work clothes and not the shorts and T-shirt I commonly wore during the school year. I had also trimmed my hair about two inches, for I had let it grow longer back at school. As I sat in class one day, it struck me that the young lady sitting next to me was the same blonde co-ed my friend had introduced me to at college. *Wow*, I thought, *She is much prettier than I remember.* I hoped with my cleaned up look she might think I was more attractive than she first thought too. We ended up dating that summer and continued doing so into the fall semester back at college.

This was my first romantic encounter in which I truly fell in love. One thing was wrong, though. My newly acquired Christian principles were being tested like never before, and I wasn't letting Christ live victoriously through our relationship. Physically, it got too advanced, and while we never had sex, I sure thought about it *a lot*. At this point in my life, I had no idea how to be a Christian leader in a relationship or what it was supposed to look like, but I did know I didn't feel right about where we were headed, so I decided toward the end of the semester to break up. It was an extremely difficult decision, for I didn't like hurting someone I still cared for deeply, but I thought I was doing the right thing.

The semester ended. I went home for Christmas break where it was wonderful reconnecting with family and old friends. On New Year's Eve, a lot of college kids were gathering at a local pub, so I went. My heart jumped to the roof when I saw my old girlfriend walk in the door. After a couple glasses of beer, the awkwardness of the situation subsided, and we became enamored with each other once again. We were never going to be separated again, and I questioned why I had broken up with her in the first place.

I was leaving for Washington DC in a couple of days to spend the spring semester at the National Institute of Health, a medical research facility, which meant I wasn't going to be able to see my girlfriend for *five* months. A virtuoso harpist started plucking my heartstrings that night, and my resistance to any temptation was trivial and weak. I knew we needed to be together. Later that night we had sex. It was my first time. Guilt, at least for this born-again believer, rolled in the next day like a steaming locomotive. I was thankful I was leaving soon for Washington DC.

A month and a half later on a cold February day in Washington DC, one of my co-op housemates told me my girlfriend was on the phone. This was prior to cell phones, so I took the call down in the basement where we could have a more intimate conversation. We started with the usual small talk, and then the biggest bomb ever to hit planet Earth, at least for me, exploded in my ear and reverberated throughout my inner core so deep I thought my heart had stopped. "I'm pregnant," she quietly but clearly stated through the earpiece.

Silence. After the longest pause of my life, I asked her how she felt and if she was sure. She was very sure. I sank deeper into the pit I was falling into. How could this happen? I mean, it was my *first time* having sex. *How unfair!* I fumed to myself. It seemed that God had played a dirty trick on me.

During the conversation, we may have mentioned marriage or doing the "right thing," but we both knew our plans didn't include this type of interruption. She mainly wanted my help to terminate the pregnancy, and I was quickly willing to oblige any way I could. She was as scared as I was. I sent her some money, and she soon had the procedure done in another city far away from our college town. I hated to admit it, but I was relieved at how the whole situation was handled. Thinking about *my* predicament and how it would affect *me* was my utmost concern that day in the basement. Worrying about the consequences of this decision or action was absent. The fact that I could think this way convicted me greatly and caused me to ask, "Am I truly a Christian?"

In Psalm 51, David reminds us of his understanding of sin and its consequences and also his appreciation of God's abundant forgiveness. David's heart agonized over the sin he had committed with Bathsheba (adultery) and later the arranged murder of her husband, Uriah. These events convicted David greatly after the prophet Nathan revealed to him that he and God knew of his acts. David knew the joy of forgiveness and also God's mercy when Nathan told him his sins had been forgiven, but there was a consequence to his action, which resulted in the death of Bathsheba's and his child.

My memory along with my poor understanding of forgiveness later caused me great anguish and fear of the consequences resulting from my sinful action. How could I be so ruthless and fearful at the same time? Needless to say, I was devastated as I sat alone in the basement that day. We made a vain attempt after I returned to college the next summer to try to salvage our relationship. It was never going to happen.

There I was, a confused nineteen-year-old college student, proclaiming I had a relationship with Christ yet deep inside carrying this horrible burden related to my recent relationship. Every day, I felt I was living a lie. The potential for God to use this event to grow my faith was enormous if I would just search for Him. But I couldn't even pray.

Future events occurred, distancing me from God, but this particular one started the insidious process. The hardening of my heart was beginning. At times, it would be briefly softened during moments of conviction and rededication, but my underlying thoughts and memories accumulated and my inability to deal with them grew.

My fear of revealing my sinfulness to other Christians was significant. It seemed to me that everyone else had "perfect" lives, and I knew they wouldn't want to associate with me if they knew of my "secret." *No one would believe I am Christian with such a history,* I thought. This immature thinking kept me from understanding God's forgiveness and the meaning of Christ's sacrifice for many years. In a distorted way, I believed Christians couldn't commit such horrible sins. Worse, I thought if they had, perhaps they were never Christian in the first place. The seed of doubt had been planted.

My spiritual heart's condition was deteriorating much like a sand castle melting away with each wave of an approaching tide. Despite its decomposing state, I was still able to maintain a "healthy" spiritual appearance to the observing world. My outward and not inward appearance was more important throughout much of my life. *How much longer can I keep juggling before everything falls to the ground?* I often wondered to myself.

Chapter 7

Warning Signs

Later that summer in 2009, after my normal cardiology workup, I kept having occasional rapid rhythms in my heart, but I thought nothing of them, for I was always asymptomatic. After all, I had received a clean bill of health from my cardiologist. The cardiac events unfolding in my life that summer reminded me of another improbable incident with particularly low odds of ever happening. This situation illustrates that when you hear and see things that don't make sense, trust your gut, and start asking questions. If you don't, you might end up viewing one of the most hilarious sites of your life.

In 1992, Cindy and I were living in Virginia, and I was working in the ER at the Portsmouth Naval Hospital. I drove to the hospital via the Midtown traffic tunnel that connected my Ghent neighborhood in Norfolk to Portsmouth. I was late for my day shift, which started at eight o'clock, so I was speeding through the tunnel. As I came out, and just before the exit to Portsmouth, a police officer pulled me over with his lights flashing. I watched through my side view mirror as he pulled his overweight, forty-something-year-old body from his black-and-white. He sauntered up to my car and asked in his Southern drawl, "Do you know how fast you were going?" I was waiting to hear "son" or "boy" at the end of his sentence, but it didn't happen.

I had an idea how fast I was going, but I didn't let him know. I was wearing my navy lieutenant commander uniform at the time, so I was hoping perhaps this navy uniformed officer would receive a little leniency from my "brethren" uniformed officer from the police. Fat chance. I told him I was late for work. He looked disgusted with my answer and started to review my driver's license and insurance paperwork while standing next to my car. As he was standing there, I experienced the most tactless roadway tradition between passing motorists and a police officer ticketing a pulled-over vehicle.

Passing cars *honked* as they drove by. *How rude*, I thought at each Doppler-effected horn honk. It's embarrassing enough to be pulled over by a cop on a busy street, but this tradition wasn't helping my situation one iota. The honking continued over and over. All I wanted at that moment was for this guy to speed up the process so I could get the heck out of there.

While waiting on the deliberately slow-paced officer, I glanced in my rearview mirror and couldn't believe my eyes. His patrol car with lights flashing was slowly rolling backward down the slightly inclined road leading toward the tunnel. Cars were *dodging* the police car and then honking as they went by my car to get the officer's attention. I turned and yelled at the officer, "Your car! It's rolling away!" He looked up from his tablet and nearly jumped out of his clothes as he immediately took off running to catch his getaway patrol car. As I said, he was quite overweight and probably hadn't passed a fitness test in years, but that day he was moving every inch of circumferential body fat as if he were an Olympic sprinter. Hilarious!

When I thought it couldn't get any better (or worse, depending how you look at it), his patrol car approximately fifty yards away jumped the curb of the median in the middle of the road. The next thing that happened couldn't have been scripted better for a movie. The median in the road was just wide and high enough to fit between the front and rear tires of the patrol car, and just like he had rolled the vehicle onto a lift at the mechanic's shop, the car was suspended with all four wheels unable to touch the street. The rear wheels spun rapidly each time he stepped on the gas.

I was now howling. I couldn't believe the odds of this ever happening to anyone getting a speeding ticket. But what does one do in this situation? I noticed the officer was sticking his left arm out his driver's window, motioning for me to move on. I didn't want to break the law by leaving the scene of a crime, but I also knew he didn't want any witnesses hanging around explaining the details of this highly embarrassing event. I could already hear the verbal jabs that officer would fend off in the break room at headquarters the next day. I began to see flashing lights from other patrol cars coming through the tunnel. I placed my car into gear and sheepishly drove away and up the exit ramp with a quiet giggle.

During the summer of 2009 in Boerne, "horn honks" were passing by again, but my cardiologist and I were not paying much attention. He was standing next to my "car" (my body) examining it along with my labs and EKGs, and I was sitting there wondering what the "horn honks" (symptoms) were all about. If only I had a rearview mirror to see why the cars were dodging one another, maybe then I would have discovered the cause for all the commotion with my heart.

My spiritual life was also filled with sirens, horn honks, and dodging cars, but I had become spiritually tone deaf and didn't know there was a rearview mirror to glance at. I didn't even know I was being pulled over.

Chapter 8

Chem 101

The normal cardiac workup I received that summer was reassuring, but it still didn't explain my problem. Yes, I had agreed my stress issues were potentially a cause, but I had a difficult time proving to myself that all the rapid heartbeats were not related to something more serious. I have taken care of many patients in the ER having MIs (myocardial infarctions), or heart attacks, who had been recently told their stress test was normal. Every physician knows that all diagnostic tests have their limits. I wondered if something was being missed in mine.

Patients who have an unusual or rare illness often have workups that don't make sense. Variables must be considered by the examining physician, and unless he considers all options, the correct diagnosis might be missed. How does a physician know when he or she is confronted with an illness that doesn't play by the normal rules? What is it that leads him or her to think outside the proverbial diagnostic box so that the more rare diagnosis is identified? I believe one of the first steps is to never be satisfied with an answer if it doesn't clearly make sense. Also, it is important to not limit the number of diagnoses at the beginning of a workup. The ultimate step is the *desire* to find the right answer. If these variables don't exist, a rare or atypical diagnosis will never be found.

My first college class was a lesson in not being fooled by a peculiar presentation. It taught me to observe, be patient, and be sure that what is seen is for real. As the adage goes, "If it's too good to be true (or too terrible to tolerate), it probably is."

I was sitting in a large amphitheater-styled classroom with approximately five hundred other freshmen at eight o'clock on a Monday morning, awaiting the arrival of my first college professor in my first college class. The tension and excitement were high. I couldn't believe I was finally in a college classroom. At precisely one second after eight o'clock, a rotund, approximately fifty-year-old fellow entered the classroom from the rear of the auditorium wearing a newly pressed white coat with his embroidered name proudly displayed over his front pocket. He marched down the stairs toward the front of the auditorium, making each deliberate step echo like a bass drum—their pace much slower than the anticipatory beats of each student's heart. He never turned his head toward the class as he approached the distant elevated podium.

Standing at the podium, he spoke with a slow, commanding cadence. "I am Dr. Rod O'Connor, chairman of the Department of Chemistry and author of the textbook sitting on your desk. I am your professor for Chemistry 101." He spoke with such authority, as if God himself were speaking through the microphone. He began to explain in intricate detail the massive amount of material we were to learn that semester. Our ears perked up when he told us that over half of the class would not pass the course.

Panic set in. Many of us had heard of this thing called Drop/Add, where a student can drop a class and switch to another in the first week of the semester. Most of my five hundred brethren were all thinking the same thing I was, *How can I get to the back door first?* The professor rambled on, each word he delivered driving a stake further and further into our now limp bodies. *This is the end of my college career, and I haven't even started,* I thought.

At this point, with all hope lost, something peculiar began to happen in that eight o'clock Chemistry 101 class at Blevins Hall. Out of thin air and much like a whisper from the academic heavens, a musical note began to emanate from the speakers overhead. *Am I hearing things?* I thought. My fellow classmates were looking around also, apparently hearing the same music, convincing me I wasn't having a psychotic break with auditory hallucinations. But where was it coming from and why?

I recognized the tune as it became louder—the Mighty Mouse theme *Saturday Night Live* comedian Andy Kaufman had made famous, declaring, "Here I come to save the day!" On the first beat of the refrain, the rear door of the classroom burst open. Silhouetted in the doorway stood a middle-aged, balding guy wearing a stuffed Superman outfit. He appeared quite Schwarzenegger-ish as he sang the well-known theme. He ran down the stairs holding a fire extinguisher that he ignited, creating white "smoke" that engulfed the professor standing on the podium. Dr. O'Connor was forced to leave the classroom through a hidden door in the wall behind the podium.

We were dumbfounded. With mouths gaping, we all wondered what had just happened. Before anyone could utter a sound, "Superman" walked up to the podium and said calmly and joyfully, "Hi, I'm Dr Bain, your *real* Chemistry 101 professor, and I'm going to tell you the *real* way Chemistry 101 is taught!" My counterparts and I jumped to our feet screaming without restraint our joy and relief. The jubilation could be heard across the entire campus. I fell back into my chair and smiled, thinking, *Maybe this isn't going to be my last day of college, after all.*

This is one of my favorite memories. I loved the creativity of my college chemistry professors and their understanding of the freshman mind and its associated anxiety that first day of college. So many things are easily forgotten in life, but special memories never leave us.

Were my cardiologist and I misinterpreting the awkward presentation of my heart rhythm problems that summer? They seemed to be growing in frequency rather than less, and I was addressing every stress issue I could imagine. As my symptoms progressed, I was wishing Superman would pop out from somewhere and assure me that everything was fine and not as it appeared. He never showed up.

Chapter 9

Expect the Unexpected

Toward the end of August on a trip to Seattle and Oregon, I began to notice I was having difficulty walking up steep hills. And on an excursion to beautiful Crater Lake, I was relieved when my friend Dale couldn't take the hike down to the lake because of a bad knee. I offered to stay up top with him so "we could spend some time together" while driving around the lake. Actually, for the first time in my life, I was concerned about my capability to perform physically, for I was afraid I wouldn't be able to climb back up from the water's edge. Now my symptoms were affecting my decision-making related to activity. I now knew something wasn't right.

After returning home from our trip to the great Pacific Northwest, I noticed my breathing was becoming slightly more labored when walking up stairs, so I started asking others to go up for me to retrieve keys and such. I know I had received a clean bill of health in June, but something was developing that wasn't right and stress was looking less likely the culprit. In medicine, a physician can do everything to evaluate and treat his patient correctly, yet disaster still strikes. It's just the way it is. It will never change.

I had an experience doing something "the right way," but *still* leading to disaster. It happened with my *first* delivery of a baby as a medical student. I was on my OB-GYN (obstetrics and gynecology) rotation during my third year of medical school, the year when each student rotates through a different service like general surgery, internal medicine, pediatrics, psychiatry, etc. every six to eight weeks. The third year of my medical school education was both brutally exhausting and exhilarating. I had to spend the night in the hospital about every fourth night, which provided ample opportunity to witness and experience many medical, surgical, and psychiatric events that would stick in my mind forever. This first on-call night in OB-GYN would be such a night.

The ER was slow that night, and there were no gynecology patients to be evaluated, so the OB-GYN resident asked, "Are you interested in delivering a baby?" Well, first of all, as a third-year medical student, you *always* respond energetically and positively when asked to do *anything* by your resident. Second, you quickly learn as much as possible from any instructional resource available about the procedure you have been asked to perform. *Oh boy, I'm going to deliver a baby!* I anxiously thought. *Am I ready? Have I had the proper training needed to do this?* Medical school training is like this. At any moment you are asked to execute a task you didn't think you were ready to perform, yet with close guidance by a resident or attending physician, you suddenly find yourself accomplishing the task, and your confidence soars. I couldn't wait to see how high mine would soar after delivering my first baby!

I went to labor and delivery about midnight and was introduced to a delightful woman who was in labor with her fourth child. The thought of delivering her baby scared me to death, but I put on the most confident air I could muster and told her I would be with her throughout the night and help deliver her child. Like the captain on the bridge of the USS *John Young* who saw my eyes fill with panic when he asked if I would ride the chair to the other ship, I'm sure the laboring mother saw a similar expression. She fortunately didn't say anything to acknowledge my fearful look, though, and for that I was appreciative. She thanked me for being there.

I hadn't enough experience or insight to realize that the laboring woman knew more about giving birth than anyone else in the room. After all, this was her *fourth* vaginal delivery. I also had forgotten that the process of birthing babies had been going on for thousands of years. If I just stayed out of the way, everything would probably work out just fine. I couldn't help but think of Prissy in *Gone With the Wind* explaining to Scarlett O'Hara, "I don't know nothin' 'bout birthin' babies!" Her facial expression was probably similar to mine, but sometimes you just have to laugh at yourself, plow through the anxieties, and trust that everything will be all right.

That night, I listened and learned a lot about obstetrics from a savvy OB nurse while working with my, or more appropriately, her patient. Doesn't matter ... I did what she told me to do. A good third-year medical student always listens carefully to a seasoned nurse, for the nurse's experience level is significantly more than any third-year medical student. The nurse can keep a medical student out of considerable trouble if he or she likes you. In other words, they can save your butt, but if they think you are arrogant or need to be taken down a notch or two, they can let you hang out to dry, causing you to look like a fool in front of the resident, or even worse, staff attending doctor. My nurse liked me, so we got along fine.

Labor progressed rapidly, and by two a.m., her cervix was fully dilated to ten centimeters, or the distance between the tips of the index and middle fingers when spread wide apart. At this point, she was ready to stop the "hee-hee-heeing" and "ho-ho-hoing" breathing she had learned in Lamaze class. This wasn't her first pony ride, so she knew it was time to push that kid out of there.

The ensuing minutes illustrated one of the most violent acts I had ever witnessed. The amount of pressure a woman can exert when desperately trying to push a baby through the vaginal opening is absolutely astounding to me and beyond words. My mentor nurse grabbed one of her legs and ordered me to take the other. We both pulled her legs back toward her chest, and she held her breath and pushed as we counted to ten. One, two, three, … ten! I thought she was going to blow her brains out the way she was straining. Her face, puffy and red while pushing with each contraction, expressed the most determined look I'd ever seen.

It wasn't long before the hair on the baby's head was showing with each breath-holding push. Seeing the presenting scalp is absolutely terrifying the first time you are responsible for a delivery. My heart raced faster and faster. That baby wanted out of there, and Mom sure wanted it out too! I felt like I was the only one who might get in the way of it happening. Oh, if the USS John Young captain could see my eyes now!

I went to medical school back in the days when moms labored in one room and then were transferred to another room appropriately called the delivery room. We rolled the gurney into the delivery room and demanded she breathe through her contractions a couple of times until we got her set up. The last thing we wanted was a baby coming out in the hallway. Poor form, you know. In the delivery room, the mother's legs are placed into the cold metal stirrups—all vanity is lost during the delivery process. Everything was moving so fast as I tried to figure out how to put on my sterile paper gown. How my nurse must have been laughing to herself while watching me awkwardly move about, but she never let on, and I was appreciative of her professional demeanor.

My resident was gowned and ready to guide me every step of the way, all the while explaining the entire birthing process. He directed my hands and helped me perform a small episiotomy (incision at the bottom of the vaginal opening) to assist the passage of the child through the final stage of delivery. Wow! It was really happening! My gloved hand was on the head, and I guided it out as Mom made a heavy push. Once the head was completely out, everyone immediately asked her to stop pushing. I suctioned the nose and mouth, and we checked for the umbilical cord around the baby's neck, as sometimes it can wrap around the neck one or two times and strangle the child if it is not loosened and unwound. It was looped around once, so I unwound the cord over the baby's head. Okay. We, no, I was ready to deliver the shoulder of the baby from under the pubic bone. The first time you do this you swear you are going to pull the baby's head off, but this little guy was tough and durable, so I commenced with the tugging. The baby exploded out of Mom and into my sterilely draped arms. Everybody yelled, "It's a boy!" In 1983, not every pregnant woman had an ultrasound during her prenatal care, so often the gender of the baby was still a surprise at delivery.

I thought I was going to drop him, for he was so slippery, but I held on tight and then performed one of the most ceremonial passages into physician-hood: the cutting of the umbilical cord. I placed a plastic clamp on the cord near the baby and then clamped Mom's side of the cord with a hemostat. I cut the cord with scissors, and suddenly, he was on his own. After the cord is cut, a baby is no longer dependent on the mother for oxygenated blood. When the child cries and fills those previously never-used lungs with air (79 percent oxygen and 21 percent nitrogen), a new source of oxygenated blood occurs.

I handed the newborn to my trusted nurse who quickly placed the baby on a warmer where she wiped him down to get the moisture off. The moisture is very cooling to the baby via the evaporation process, so getting it off is critical to maintain warmth and avoid hypothermia. She immediately determined APGAR scores (assessment technique for evaluating the health of a newborn). The baby was a little blue, so she applied oxygen to his face to pink him up. This happens often, I had heard, so nothing to worry about.

Well, there I was gently pulling on the hemostats clamped around the cord, waiting for the placenta to release itself from the inner lining of the uterus. My resident physician could see the excitement and exhilaration in my eyes as I peeked over the edge of my facemask. *I am becoming a doctor,* I thought, *and I love it!*

I looked over at the warmer and noticed that the newborn was getting bluer, even with oxygen. The nurse was getting anxious, and we all heard the baby's heartbeat being tapped out on the edge of the warmer by another nurse's finger. As the pulse dropped lower and lower, the nurse slapped a button on the wall, which directly sent a signal to the neonatal intensive care unit (NICU). Within seconds, the pediatric resident assigned to work the NICU was in our room. He took one look at the baby and immediately scooped him up into his arms and exited through a door at the rear of the delivery room that was connected directly to the NICU.

I thought, *This certainly seems odd.* The mom asked what was wrong, and I explained to her from my *vast* experience, "Sometimes babies have difficulty breathing and need more attention by the doctor in the NICU where they can better care for the baby." I assured her, "Do not worry." The OB-GYN resident and I delivered the placenta and then repaired the episiotomy. We quickly transferred her to the postpartum area, and off we went to the NICU to check on the baby.

The NICU staff, including the pediatric resident I had seen in the delivery room, was huddled closely around a warmer. It was an eerie site, for at night the NICU nursing staff turns down the ceiling lights, making the unit quite dark. The NICU team seemed aglow while standing under the warmer's lights in the darkened NICU as they worked on the baby I had proudly delivered moments before. As I approached the NICU team, the chief pediatric resident stepped back from the warmer, removed his gloves, and said, "That's it. Let's call it." The phrase, Let's call it, is used by a doctor after he or she has expended all resuscitative efforts. The patient is then pronounced dead.

This was the child I had just delivered! My *first* delivery! "This *cannot* be happening!" I gasped. What did I do? Terrified, I grabbed the pediatric resident's arm and asked, "What are you doing?" When he looked at me, I could tell that he was wondering who I was, but I didn't care. My first delivery had just died, and I knew I must have been responsible. Absolute fear was expressed all over my face. The OB-GYN resident could only say, "I'm sorry." I asked him what happened, but he didn't have an answer.

The pediatric NICU resident had no explanation for the baby's death either. As the staff drifted away, I stood in the dark room next to the dead baby's illuminated body not believing the sight upon which I was gazing. What had happened? What had I done?

The OB-GYN resident told me to take the rest of the night off and to go to the on-call room. It was about three a.m. The resident delivered the awful news to the mom, and while I felt I should go with him, I was relieved he went alone. I'm sure the mystified look on my face wouldn't have been consoling to her; plus, I think the resident thought I had been shell-shocked enough for one night. I went to the smelly multi-bunk on-call room where residents and medical students try to sleep when spending the night at the hospital. I found an empty bed, not knowing who had slept there previously, and laid down, thinking about all that had transpired. I didn't sleep a wink. All I could think about was how my medical career was probably already over, and I hadn't even completed the third year of medical school! Where was the "Mighty Mouse" chemistry professor who could "save the day?"

Six a.m. rolled around quickly. I was exhausted after not sleeping. I made rounds with my OB-GYN resident, and afterward, we went to the conference room where the entire attending physician staff, residents, interns, and medical students of the OB-GYN department were sitting and preparing for the morning conference.

This particular OB-GYN meeting occurring immediately after my catastrophic delivery was appropriately named the "M&M Conference," which stands for morbidity and mortality, and is the most important conference of the month for any medical or surgical service. This is the conference in which the entire attending staff discusses a patient(s) who had a poor outcome during the previous month. "Wow, what timing," I quietly agonized to myself. I couldn't have scripted my demise more perfectly.

The head of the OB-GYN department decided that the child I had delivered just four hours earlier was so interesting that it would be the lone case discussed at today's M&M. I could hear the trigger being cocked. I was about to face the firing squad, and all that was left for me to do was take a puff of my last cigarette. I didn't smoke, but I think I could have started that day.

Fortunately for me, the OB-GYN resident presented the case. Thank You, God! They went over the mom's prenatal history, labor, and delivery in painstaking detail. No stone was unturned. I sank deeper and deeper into my seat, willing the day to come to an end. I knew at any second that I was going to hear my name called out, and then I would have to explain what had happened earlier that morning at two a.m. I had never felt such dread in all my life. Once again the look of fear returned to my face, much like the one that was there with the captain of the USS *John Young* and in the basement while on the phone with my pregnant girlfriend.

Jesus said to Simon, "Don't be afraid; from now on you will catch men." (Luke 5:10) after Simon had observed the miraculous catch of fish filling his nets after Jesus had told him to throw his nets into the water even though they had been empty the night before. David wrote, "Even though I walk through the valley of the shadow of death, I will fear no evil, for you are with me; your rod and your staff, they comfort me." (Psalm 23:4) The phrase "do not fear" is mentioned in the Bible 365 times, and Jesus knows that we all struggle with fear. He illustrated through his sacrifice on the cross that we don't have to any more. Since my life had strayed from Christ during this period of my life, any comfort or safe haven from fear seemed far away.

After an exhaustive discussion, the head of the OB-GYN department concluded he saw nothing that had been done inappropriately. *What? Did I hear him right? Certainly they are missing something.* I knew, even at the third-year medical student level, which is the lowest level on the doctor totem pole, it is not normal for a healthy-appearing baby to die at delivery. I knew I had done something wrong with this kid, and no one was going to convince me otherwise.

The rest of the attending OB-GYN staff *agreed* with the department head. *Oh my God, I'm acquitted!* The jury had spoken. I couldn't believe it, but I still felt miserable and responsible. The final verdict was still out, for the autopsy was pending. I wouldn't rest until I heard that report.

Not allowing myself to be guiltless even when fault can't be found was a recurring issue for me. I always looked at myself first when something went awry, for unfortunately, I always thought I was the most likely cause of the problem. Where did this thinking come from? Had my self-worth reached such an abyss that I could not see Christ in me? Where was the joy? Where was the freedom? Why was I not experiencing it daily? This is where I had finally sunk in my spiritual life, and the pit at times seemed too deep to climb out of on my own.

The distorted perception I had developed of my relationship with Christ started innocently with a seed of doubt that was inserted into my thinking after I had committed what I thought was a "special" sin. Not understanding the forgiveness that comes from accepting Christ as my Savior, my doubt grew into an entangled, thorny bush of wrong, critical thinking and an increasing separation from God.

I knew I couldn't live in this world without sinning, but although I understood Christ's sacrifice for those sins, I still felt inadequate in my relationship to God. I knew my sins were forgiven, but shouldn't there have been more change in my life than what I'd seen? I clearly knew of my extreme inadequacy and absolute need for Him. He had revealed His loving grace to me at seventeen, but I elected to ignore so many of His truths and promises. I kept struggling with the guilt of my past and my inability to understand the abundance of mercies Christ had shown me—mercies that covered all sins past, present, and future. I wouldn't allow myself to be forgiven and had been flogging myself for years. My lack of understanding His forgiveness made me feel guilty *before* any adverse event occurred in my life. I didn't understand that I have been guilty since the day I was born, and that freedom only occurs upon accepting Christ. I thought I had gained this freedom at age seventeen, but since then, for some reason I increasingly felt more captive. Why did it seem I was guiltier *after* I became a Christian?

A hollow, empty feeling developed in my gut, and I felt like ending my career that day in the OB-GYN department. I desperately needed counseling, but there was none, and I didn't go looking for it either. I had too much pride to admit that this was too tough for me to handle. So I just swallowed it down like a bitter pill and accepted it as just a part of the "experience" of medical school.

I think this particular episode illustrated to me the cold nature of medical training, for no one from the OB-GYN staff counseled or discussed with me my horrific experience from my first delivery. *This is the way it is in medical training, so I had better get tough around the edges,* I thought. This is one of the reasons why so many young physicians become cynical and calloused before they ever start private practice.

The autopsy result came in three days later. I had been waiting on pins and needles each day, dreading the detailed pathologist's description of what I had done wrong. The baby ended up having bilateral Bochdalek hernias. These are literally holes on each side of the diaphragm (the muscle under both lungs that separates the abdomen from the thoracic cavity). Bochdalek hernias occur in 1:2,200–12,500 births, increased in males, and 25–60 percent die at birth. (Jeffrey, Mark E., and Wilbur A. Gorodetsky. "Adult Bochdalek Hernia." Medind. 10, Sept. 2004, accessed June 12, 2011).

These are often not diagnosed until birth. This child's intestines had moved into the chest cavity, and his lungs had never developed. He didn't have a chance to live once the umbilical cord was cut, for when the cord was severed, his only one way to receive oxygenated blood was through his own lungs. Lungs he did not have.

I thought it ironic that my very first opportunity to cut an umbilical cord, the one procedure that releases a totally dependent life into the world, would end up being the one act that initiated the demise of my first delivery. I knew for certain I had nothing to do with causing the infant's death after hearing the pathologist's report, but I still had a raw feeling in the pit of my stomach. I wondered, "What are the odds of a medical student delivering their first baby and it ending up dying within minutes?" This level of statistical probability was not the first nor last in my life.

"Why did this happen to me?" I questioned. Instead of searching for an answer in the only source for truth, God's Word, I continued my wayward thinking. I often thought about my first sexual experience and how it ended and questioned if my involvement with this child's birth was related in some way. Would I continue to suffer the consequences of this unforgiveable sin from my past? "Another 'first' resulting in a death," I agonized. What were the odds?

My first delivery illustrated how medical practitioners can be flawless in their execution, yet disaster still strikes with an amazing sting. There is nothing anyone can do to stop such occurrences. My previous cardiac workup in Boerne by my cardiologist was performed without flaw, but I wondered, "Is something catastrophic heading my way?" My symptoms suggested the possibility. I would find out soon enough.

Chapter 10

I Really Do Have a Heart Problem

The winds were changing that fall of 2009 with each cool front blowing in. I continued noticing my difficulty in climbing stairs at home, for each step I was now pausing to catch my breath. Despite the changes that were developing, I was still able to work in the clinics and go about my usual daily tasks, but I knew something wasn't right. What would it take to get me to seek help?

While eating lunch with my family at a local sandwich shop, I felt lightheaded. I checked my left radial pulse; it was pulsating at *thirty-two* beats per minute and was irregular. *This is not good*, I thought to myself. Not wanting to alarm my family, I finished my meal, stood up slowly, and then exited the restaurant without fanfare. I told Cindy as I was driving home that I needed to go to the clinic, for I was noticing some irregular heartbeats, and that maybe I could capture the rhythm on an EKG. My driving and carrying on with my duties while developing a potentially life-threatening heart rhythm is not something I am proud of, but when faced with my own severe medical situation, all reasonable thought went out the door. It is amazing how I justified these ridiculous acts during these symptomatic episodes.

I entered my urgent care clinic in Boerne and sat on a gurney near the heart monitor. After removing my shirt, one of the staff nurses applied the EKG leads. Paper rolled off the machine, and with a sudden "rip," she tore the EKG off and handed it to me. I stared at my EKG revealing a second-degree AV heart block, Mobitz type II. To the nonmedical person, that doesn't mean much, but to an ER doctor, it means a lot and the potential for where this rhythm could lead, even more.

I need to take a moment to give you a short medical school lesson in "heart rhythm anatomy 101." The heart normally beats at a rate between sixty and one hundred bpm when not stressed. It can go slower or higher, depending on the conditioning of the person and whether they are on medications that affect the heart rate; if they have an illness that influences the heart rate like hyperthyroidism; if they are excited, exercising, or have a fever; or if they have an inherent problem with the electrical conducting system of the heart. This last condition I want to discuss in more detail.

The electrical system of the heart is not wires and a generator, but analogously, it consists of special heart cells that respond to one another by allowing different elements like calcium, sodium, and potassium to be transferred across their membranes in a way that allows for a very low voltage potential to flow from the originating beat in the SA node located in

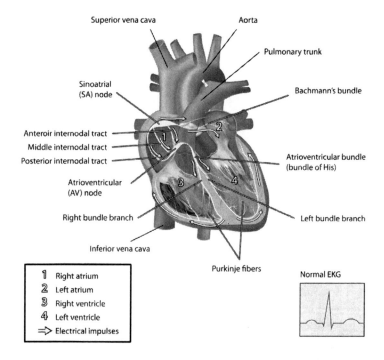

With Permission Peter Junaidy | Dreamstime.com

Diagram of Electrical System of Heart

the right atrium to the remainder of the heart. Once this electrical "potential" is started, its current is conducted down the special cells to the rest of the muscle cells in the atria, causing each to contract and pump blood into the ventricles (lower chambers of the heart). The atrial electrical current is then captured in another gathering spot (node) called the AV (atrioventricular) node that is located between the right atrium and right ventricle. The AV node recognizes the new current and transmits it to a special group of cells organized in the ventricle region called the His-Purkinje system. This "conduit" transmits the current rapidly throughout the ventricles and ignites the rest of the ventricles' heart muscle cells to contract, resulting in blood being pumped to the aorta and lungs from the left and right ventricles, respectively.

In a nutshell, this is how the heart conducts its "electrical" current and creates contractions of the heart. Anything that interrupts this flow through the electrical system, depending at which point the interruption occurs, can cause serious and some not-so-serious electrical abnormalities of the heart called arrhythmias.

My second-degree, Mobitz type II AV heart block meant I was conducting (transmitting) my electrical currents intermittently through the AV node located between my right atrium and right ventricle. This resulted in my ventricles beating slower than my atria (pleural for atrium), and thus the pulse in my wrist was slow too, for my pulse reflects *ventricular* contractions. Intermittent atrial pulses were being conducted through the AV node to the ventricle. As long as enough transmissions to the ventricles were occurring, I was able to remain alert and upright by maintaining an acceptable blood pressure. If the number of beats transmitted decreased, I would develop increasing lightheadedness and potentially pass out.

I was able to maintain a systolic (upper number) blood pressure above ninety with my ventricles beating at thirty-two bpm, but I didn't want to wait and see how long I could keep it up, so I contacted my electrophysiologist (EP), who is a cardiologist specially trained to manage heart rhythm problems. He admitted me to the hospital, and the following day, an ablation procedure was attempted because of my history of intermittent rapid heart rates that I had noted earlier in the summer, which, until now, were thought to be primarily caused by stress.

Cardiac ablation is a procedure in which a catheter is placed into a large blood vessel(s) in one or both groins and guided to the right atrium or left ventricle. The electrophysiologist "maps out" the internal surface of a ventricle, atrium, or both on the left and/or right sides of the heart. I won't talk about ablations to the epicardium (outside surface of the heart), which is accessed through the skin of the upper abdomen. The mapping procedure pinpoints locations where abnormal rapid heart rhythms originate. Once identified, a special catheter delivers a low-voltage current to the "mapped out" site and burns the superficial lining of the heart (or endocardium). This results in a "burned out" segment that doesn't allow an aberrant electrical impulse to cross or originate.

During the three-hour procedure, my electrophysiologist couldn't identify the focus, or origin, of my rapid heart rate. After he discussed his findings with Cindy in the waiting room, a pacemaker was inserted to keep my heart from beating too slow, but I would also need to take medicine in the future to prevent my heart rate from going too fast. As you can see, I didn't know which side was up or down at this point with my heart. One day it would beat too fast, the next too slow. My spiritual life was a little like this too. One day I would feel close to God and the next far away. Where was the regularity? Where was the consistency?

Well, I guess I really do have a heart problem, I thought. Why had it deteriorated to the point of needing a pacemaker? Why did I have this problem in the first place? The answer I received was, "I don't know. Some individuals just seem to get these problems after fifty years of age, and we don't know why." I accepted that and became determined to live a normal life with my new Medtronic pacemaker, which allowed me to feel normal again. At home, I was able to climb stairs without hesitating, and after just a few weeks, I was back in the driver's seat, going full throttle again!

Chapter 11

Running the Wrong Race

My first salute as an active duty navy physician occurred one sunny morning while walking the grounds of Balboa Naval Hospital in beautiful San Diego, California. I had just graduated from medical school and was starting my internship (first year of training after medical school) in obstetrics and gynecology. Yeah, I know, I still can't believe it either, given my experience with my first delivery. But I liked the endocrine/infertility component of the specialty, so I decided to go for it.

The first day checking in to a new duty station in the navy is spent going from building to building, department to department, carrying a piece of paper that contains a list of places you must visit. Personnel from each department then check off their appropriate box on the paper, indicating you were informed of their department's services. By the end of the day, you could prove you were checked in. I'm sure it was important to have this process done correctly, but to a recent civilian (nonmilitary) fresh out of medical school, it was a pain in the neck.

At the end of the checking-in ritual, I handed my paper to a very junior enlisted staff person at the base's administration office. She looked quite pleased that this brand-new officer had completed his mechanical task, or maybe she was just pleased I had to do it, period. Oh well, let it go, I say.

I had visited the uniform shop the day before I checked in. Since I had never had the opportunity to go to Officer Indoctrination School (OIS), where new officers learn how to dress, salute, and basically get indoctrinated into navy life, I was at the mercy of a delightful Filipino lady who helped me dress like a Navy Medical Corps officer in my summer white uniform with all the appropriate attachments. I told the uniform shop lady that I was a doctor in the United States Navy with the rank of lieutenant and needed to look the part. In her strong accent, she replied, "No problem, Doc."

The next morning while checking in to the command appropriately dressed in my summer whites, I noticed in the distance a highly decorated naval officer approaching in full regalia. He looked like the CNO (chief naval officer) himself. "Oh boy," I nervously moaned to myself. "Why did I get an admiral to be my first salute as an active duty doc? When do I salute? How do I salute appropriately? Oh well, I'll do the best I can." As the distinguished gentleman approached, I waited until he was about ten feet away, and then I jerked my right hand quickly to the brim of my hat and awaited his return salute. At that moment, I felt quite mystified as the "highly ranked" officer bent over, held his knees, and laughed (no, *howled* is more like it) at the top of his lungs. No doubt I had done something wrong, and now I was going to pay.

I stood there awkwardly, waiting to hear what I had done to warrant such an outburst of absolute humiliation. The gentleman lifted himself while wiping away tears and said, "Doc, I'm supposed to salute *you*!" He then started belly laughing again. Yes, he was a master chief petty officer, the most senior ranked *enlisted* in the navy. In the military, there are officers and enlisted. The officers get to be administrators and run the show and be bosses. The enlisted are lower in rank, and while they really run the navy, they allow the officers to boss them around. The master chief had so many ribbons on his chest and stripes down his arm I assumed he was worth saluting. In other words, I had no idea he was enlisted. I told him I had such respect for his uniform and awards that I felt I needed to salute him. He patted me on the shoulder and offered me a good day. I am sure he had a ball later that day sharing with all the chiefs in the chief's mess about how the new doc had saluted him first. I was just thankful I hadn't ticked off a highly ranked officer.

Life is like that, it seems. Creating inordinate respect for things in the wrong order. Saluting entities you *think* are most important, only to find out later you weren't supposed to salute them at all. I saluted the wrong guy in San Diego because I hadn't been to OIS, where I would have learned the hierarchy of saluting. Similarly, I had neglected my Christian training by not regularly seeking God's guidance or filling my mind with His invaluable teaching. Ignoring His lead had whittled down my ability to discern and make critical decisions consistent with His teaching. I abandoned my training as a Christian during these years and became clueless with respect to what I should "salute" spiritually. As a result, I made mistakes and was digging a deeper pit.

In the spring of 2010 in Boerne, after my October pacemaker placement,

I began "saluting" another poorly prioritized entity. I was continuing to improve physically, was vigorously exercising, and had begun a new exercise program oriented to the teachings of a book called *Younger Next Year* by Chris Crowley. I believed the book could help me attain what I thought were unattainable goals physically, with or without a pacemaker. Its pages became my new gospel for living a longer life and with more vigor. I was so enthralled with the book's message that I openly shared its pages with many others at the YMCA where I worked out five to six times a week. I was creating a "Younger Next Year" fan club, and I was its most ardent fan.

It felt odd being able to exercise because of two wires—one leading to my right atria, the other to my right ventricle, and both attached to an electrical generator. My life's physical dependence had been transferred to this unique device, but my spiritual dependence seemed to be losing its "pacemaker" altogether. It seemed I was growing less dependent on God each day, never realizing my need for Him was growing stronger than ever before.

I was focusing on what *I* could do to increase my health and well-being. I wasn't going to let a little heart thing slow *me* down. I had been threatened in October, and my knee-jerk response was to fight back with all I had. My mind wasn't focused on Christ, and when stress or trials came, I took off on my own, adopting new gods (idols) to worship, instead of growing in my faith and letting God guide me through landmines that lay ahead. My health had been keenly threatened, and I wasn't sure why, but I was going to make sure it didn't defeat me. I began running *my* good race with vigor. The only problem was, I was running on the wrong track.

Chapter 12

Working Out at the YMCA (or Hoofbeats)

By March, I was exercising daily at the YMCA and following my *Younger Next Year* exercise plan. I felt great!

One day while lying supine, or on my back, on a weight bench, a young woman approached and asked while staring down at me, "Are you a doctor?" This is a question a physician answers cautiously, for he or she never knows why it is being asked, but of course I said, "Yes, I am." With a gentle calmness, she explained, "A man has fallen off the stair climber and is now lying face down on the floor."

I got up as fast as I could and noticed a crowd of people huddled around the man. I rushed over and yelled, "I am a physician!" with the most authoritative, deep voice I could muster. They politely separated and created an opening, which revealed the corpse-like being lying motionless on the carpeted floor. The crowd had closely gathered around the man to assess his status, but they were very careful not to touch him for fear of doing something wrong. One individual was painstakingly down on all fours with his face next to the floor to see if the man was breathing. This is a situation the average person doesn't see very often, so knowing what to do doesn't come naturally.

His pale, lifeless face with blood-stained lips activated the emergency medicine physician within me. Realizing he was in dire straits, I rolled him over onto his back and noticed his urine-soaked shorts. This associated with blood on his lips led me to consider the possibility of a seizure. I wondered if he was postictal, the state people temporarily go into after a seizure that often resembles death to the casual observer. If that were the case, he would come around soon enough, but as I felt for a pulse through his urine-soaked shorts over the femoral artery located in his groin area, I determined the reason for his demise. He had *no pulse*. He also wasn't breathing. I asked if 911 had been called, and the staff answered yes. I then asked if anyone knew CPR. A stocky young man who looked like he had been waiting for this opportunity his whole life stepped up and confidently said, "I do!" "Great!" I responded, and CPR commenced.

I next asked if the YMCA had an AED (automatic external defibrillator), to which a staff member answered, "Yes, and I happen to be the AED trainer for the Y!" *How perfect*, I thought with a smile. She retrieved the AED and applied the leads efficiently and precisely to the patient's bare chest. The AED automatically read the rhythm and announced in its mechanized but authoritative voice, "Stand back." This older unit required one of us to press the button, which would shock (defibrillate) the patient. *Nobody* wanted to touch that button, so I slammed it down, and a jolt of electricity penetrated the dying man's chest.

The over two hundred-pound man vaulted into the air three to four inches from the carpeted floor. He developed a pulse and started to wake up, though very confused and combative from the temporary anoxia (no oxygen) to his brain. He tried to sit up and, with the voice of a baritone opera singer, began screaming and moaning at the top of his lungs. I restrained him, but before he sat up completely, he became unconscious and collapsed to the floor. CPR commenced once more.

Again, the AED was activated since the man had probably reverted to a bad rhythm. He was shocked a second time; again the loud moaning erupted with the associated combativeness. This process recurred a third time. The YMCA members who had been working out were now gathered at the water fountain far away from the scene. Most were probably witnessing their very first cardiac resuscitation and were probably thinking to themselves, *Why is that man (me) torturing him so?* when they heard each agonizing moan after he was shocked. I couldn't worry about what the crowd was thinking, though, for this man was seriously trying to die, and if I didn't do something quickly, he was going to be successful.

After what seemed like hours but were actually only minutes later, the EMS unit arrived at the scene. I could now look at a monitor of the patient's heart and see what type of rhythm he was in. Ah, there it was. Ventricular tachycardia (V tach), but it wasn't a routine V tach. It was torsade de pointes, a special variation of V tach in which the rhythm literally looks like a corkscrew on the monitor. (See next page for diagrams of EKG rhythms) V tach is bad enough and can kill quickly, but this type was more ominous and required additional treatment with a mineral (cation) called magnesium in addition to the usual medication, amiodarone.

I needed to get these drugs into his body rapidly. The EMS crew was struggling with getting an IV started, so I asked if they had an intraosseous (IO) needle available. They did, so I directed them to use it. An IO needle is literally shot from a gun-like device that inserts the needle into the tibia (leg bone) about six inches below the knee and into the bone marrow. This particular IO unit was invented and developed by an old colleague of mine, Dr Larry Miller. Thanks, Larry. Once the needle enters the bone marrow, drugs can be injected into the bloodstream where they are transferred to organs like the heart.

After injecting the drugs, I shocked him a fourth time, knowing this would be the one that would work. Like the previous three episodes, the man quickly converted and became combative, but again, he passed out shortly thereafter. I knew I just needed more time to circulate the drugs to the heart, so we performed very rigorous chest compressions for about sixty seconds. You could hear ribs cracking. I tried shocking him a fifth time. The drugs must have gotten to the heart, for this time his heart rhythm didn't go back to V tach.

Once stabilized and breathing on his own, he was hoisted onto the EMS litter, moaning every step of the way. He was rolled out to the waiting ambulance and was transported to a nearby emergency room. A doctor friend of mine was working in the ER that day, so I called him to let him know what had happened. He was appreciative and was going to have a helicopter waiting to transport him to a nearby San Antonio hospital where he would have a cardiac catheterization (cath) and possibly a cardiac stent placed.

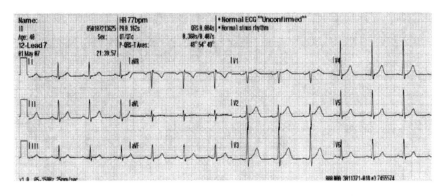

EKG example of a Normal Sinus Rhythm (a normal heart rhythm)

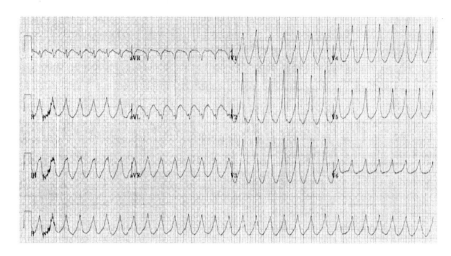

EKG example of Ventricular Tachycardia (V Tach)

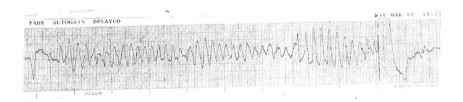

Monitor tracing of V Tach (torsade de points)

"Well, that was quite a workout," I breathed with a big sigh of relief. After the ambulance had gone, I went back inside the building, where two women approached me who had observed the climactic event. They seemed distressed and puzzled. One of them asked, "What do we do?" I wasn't sure what to tell them. She then informed me that she was the man's wife! I had been so involved in the resuscitation, I didn't think to ask if any family member was present. Her facial expression was one I had witnessed all to often in the ER—confusion and fear. Her husband had nearly died before her very eyes a couple of minutes ago while working out at the YMCA. All those thoughts, memories, and questions jam-packed into a few short minutes, all while not knowing from second to second if this was going to be the end of her husband's life and her life as she knew it. All these thoughts flooded her mind while anticipating a sudden loneliness that would be far worse than she had ever known. I tell my children, "It's what you do each and every day that prepares one's mind to handle the challenges that come suddenly." *Our reactions to stress are tempered by the disciplines of our daily lives.*

I gently explained to the man's wife the next steps related to his medical care and where he was being transported. I think she heard me, but at such times, all senses aren't firing correctly, so I hoped she at least knew where to go. I could feel her pain that day and felt quite sorry for her. As all good physicians do at such a time, I reminded her, "He is still living and battling the best he knows how. He needs you more than ever right now."

Later that week, I heard through the grapevine that my YMCA patient was eating breakfast the next morning, talking and laughing with friends and family. A stent had been placed in the left anterior descending (LAD) coronary (heart) artery known as the "widow-maker," so-called because when acutely obstructed it often kills the stricken patient, who is usually male. Many would say he was lucky that day, but luck had nothing to do with it.

I often witnessed this type of near tragedy in the ER. Sometimes it went well, like at the YMCA. Other times, not. My approach to treatment is always the same, and while never being totally sure if a patient will respond to my efforts, I know what I need to do. There are other factors in the room I have to respect, which include the patient's mind and his or her desire to live, the body and its capability to live, the spirit and its willingness to live, and, of course, God. I cannot change what is inevitable for any patient. My job as an emergency physician is to resuscitate according to how I have been trained. I always understand the limits of my actions.

These near-tragic experiences flow in and out of ERs every day, causing physicians and ER staff to protect themselves by utilizing coping mechanisms that allow maintenance of a certain level of sanity by the end of a shift. My response to these stressors resulted in a degree of detachment that protected me from not getting too lost in the sinusoidal wave of emotions. I often wondered, "How will I react when faced with a tragedy of my own? What will be my response when I cannot detach from the personal side of the resuscitation? What disciplines in my life do I partake daily that will influence my response to tragedy?" What disciplines indeed?

I often heard family members of patients say "God is good" when their relative's life was saved, but a similar refrain would be absent when death occurred. I was always frustrated by this, for wasn't God *always* good? Events in life, good or bad, are used by God to illustrate His glory and power. He uses a trial as a catalyst to stimulate inert lives to react and finally deal with sinfulness and lack of faith. He uses these catalysts to facilitate the release we need from our vaulted doubts and guilt. If we look to God when challenged, our faith is enriched, and we grow in our relationship with Him. Such trials or sufferings produce perseverance, character, and hope as stated in Romans 5:3–4. Our fear of death recedes as our dependence on Him increases.

We all must face this ultimate tragedy known as death. *Am I prepared for it? How will I react when I know it's about to happen? How will I die? What am I sure of and hope for?* Such thoughts come flooding in when faced directly with this event. I wonder what thoughts my YMCA patient and his wife had as they dealt with their sudden view of life's end?

I was glad my heart problem wasn't as bad as the YMCA patient's that day. I didn't have to think about how life ends, for I knew I was still capable of living robustly and becoming "younger next year" with my pacemaker. "Life is still good," I reminded myself as the faint sound of hoofbeats grew in the distance.

Chapter 13

Totally Out of Control

I was driving to my Bulverde clinic on May 5, a delightful spring morning a few weeks after the resuscitation at the YMCA. The air was crisp with the jubilation of spring erupting across the rolling hills. As I drove, I reflected on how I was getting into the best shape of my life by following the guidelines of my new bible, *Younger Next Year*. I was eating better and losing weight too. *Life is quite beautiful*, I thought as I pulled into the parking lot.

I stepped from my car and gathered my stethoscope and briefcase. I jogged up the nine concrete steps behind the clinic as I usually do, but when I got to the top, I felt quite lightheaded. I leaned into the side of the building, pausing to see if it would pass. It didn't.

I walked into the clinic and immediately sat down at my desk before saying hello to the staff. I rested a few minutes until the sweatiness and lightheadedness slowly dissipated. The symptoms were similar to those I had had at my Boerne clinic two days prior after climbing a couple of stairs, but this episode was much worse. "Perhaps it's time to tune up my pacemaker," I reasoned. "I'll contact my electrophysiologist in a couple of days when I am less busy." Feeling normal again, I got up from my desk and said hello to the clinic staff without telling them of my episode. I didn't need to worry them with such trivial details. We visited for a while before the second patient of the day checked in at the front desk. The clinic's *first* patient had already arrived, but he was clueless about his symptoms or need for a physician's care. But he'd learn soon enough.

I began seeing patients. While visiting with one of them later that morning, my lightheadedness recurred without warning. As beads of sweat formed on my forehead, I struggled to maintain my attention as I listened to my patient's complaint. I knew I needed to get out of there. I abruptly concluded the discussion and informed him that I'd be right back after I wrote him a prescription. I knew I was feeling desperate when I left the exam room, for I never performed an exam.

My clinic had a heart monitor and an EKG, so I had my staff place leads on my body that were attached to the heart monitor. After a few seconds, the monitor displayed a normal-paced rhythm. *That's good since I have a pacemaker,* I thought. All seemed fine, but since I had become asymptomatic when I checked my rhythm with the heart monitor, I left the leads on my chest, arms, and legs and told my staff, "If this happens again, I'll rush out of the patient's room and quickly place myself on the monitor to see if I can capture the rhythm disturbance that's causing my symptoms." They agreed jokingly, as they pictured me rushing out of an exam room and jumping onto the gurney. Wouldn't you know it? My symptoms subsided.

An hour later during a lull in clinic activity, I noted I was no longer lightheaded nor having irregular heartbeats. Having time to investigate my problem further, I thought I would do what any sane person would do. Since climbing the stairs earlier that morning had caused my symptoms to ignite, why not try it again?

My staff watched with question marks stamped on their foreheads as I marched outside through the back door and then trotted down the stairs and marched back up. Now, I am no rocket scientist, but I'm not stupid either. Well, not until this particular day. Up the steps I bounded. Immediately, my symptoms returned as I stumbled toward the gurney adjacent to the heart monitor, all the time wondering, "What kind of idiot am I?" I was pale, weak, diaphoretic (sweaty), and lightheaded as I lay there, getting connected to the monitor. My previously placed leads were connected to the monitor one by one.

Slowly, like an old black-and-white TV from the 1960s, the monitor screen began to display my rhythm. The nurse, radiology tech, and medical assistant stared motionless as the rhythm began to glow. A deafening silence consumed the clinic. We couldn't believe our eyes. I was in ventricular tachycardia, or V tach, just like my YMCA patient.

If a patient of mine presents to the clinic in V tach and is pale, diaphoretic, and lightheaded, I immediately start an IV, apply defibrillator pads to the chest and leads to connect them to a monitor, give him or her oxygen, and quickly inject the drug amiodarone—a process I had performed countless times in the ER. But again, I said if it were a *patient* of mine. On May 5, 2010, I was no one's patient, for I was the only doctor in the clinic that morning. I lay there, paralyzed, staring at the monitor in total disbelief. "There is no way I can be in V tach," I tried convincing myself. "V tach *kills* people, and I am not *ready* to die!"

Just like the wife of my YMCA patient who was hit suddenly with thoughts related to death, loneliness, and having no control, I was impacted by the same thoughts and fears crashing in with billowing waves. My heart was out of control. This was extensively more serious than any of the cardiologists or I had originally thought, for V tach requires an abnormality in the *ventricles*. *My ventricles are fine*, I thought. "What do I do?" I whispered to myself as I saw the terrified looks on the faces of my staff.

The nurse asked if I wanted to call an ambulance to which I sternly replied, "NO!" *Think, think, think*, I implored myself. Then, out of total desperation, I performed the most reckless reasoning. While evaluating my predicament and grasping for any logical explanation that could explain my problem, I made my mind up that my rhythm *had* to be an aberrantly conducted rhythm (not through the normal pathways of the heart), which originated in my pacemaker and *mimicked* V tach. I'd just wait for this episode to end, go about my day, and let the electrophysiologist know it was time to come in for a pacemaker checkup. There! No reason to call EMS or get all flustered. "This isn't V tach! This is a pacemaker problem," I confidently deducted. Boy, was I stupid.

My panicked irrational reasoning made total sense to me that day as I desperately searched for a more benign etiology causing my symptoms. My explanation had been neatly bundled into the most horrific, manipulated, obscene justification I have ever imagined any one could concoct, but there I was, taking it hook, line, and sinker, believing every word.

Minimizing signs and symptoms by patients who are worried they might have a serious disease commonly occurs when their physician is evaluating them, for they want to guide the doctor to a more benign diagnosis. The doctor has to be aware of this behavior and make sure it doesn't influence his or her decision. Here I was, believing every benign justification I could muster in order to get me out of trouble. Oh well, I was just your "average" patient, sitting in a clinic, having a life threatening arrhythmia, wondering, "When is that doctor going to show up?"

Five, ten minutes passed. Finally, the heartbeats reverted back to a normal pacemaker rhythm. *Ahhh, now I'm back to normal*, I thankfully thought. *Well, that was certainly a scare.* I took a copy of my EKG and faxed it to the office of my electrophysiologist (EP) cardiologist, but he was busy in a procedure and couldn't read it immediately.

I thought, *Since my symptoms are becoming more frequent and prolonged, I'd better have my partner come take over my shift.* While waiting for him to arrive, I did what any "normal" physician would do: I saw more patients.

To this day, I don't know what I was thinking, but there I was, discussing patients' complaints while I had just teetered on death's doorstep in V tach for ten minutes while lying on a gurney in the exam room next door. After seeing two more patients, I noticed my symptoms returned. I sat in the nurse's station, pale and sweaty. My staffs' eyes grew wider than before, and their hearts were pumping almost as fast as my 176 bpm. I can't believe I placed them in such a precarious situation.

After about ten minutes, my heart rate settled down again, and my partner arrived. He immediately started seeing patients after I explained to him I was only having problems with my pacemaker. I started feeling better, so while he was in an exam room, I performed the most idiotic (and you thought they couldn't get worse) act of my life. I left the clinic, got in my car, and drove to my EP cardiologist's office *thirty-five* minutes away in San Antonio. Any patient of mine with similar symptoms would have been transported immediately via ambulance with sirens screaming and no questions asked. Why wasn't my doctor telling me the same thing? A doctor treating himself is a *very dangerous thing*, I have discovered.

There I was, driving to the electrophysiology (EP) cardiologist's office after two prolonged episodes of V tach, hoping I wouldn't develop more symptoms along the way. Fortunately, by God's grace, I didn't. About five minutes before arriving to the office, I received a phone call.

"Brian, are you there?" It was my EP doc, relieved I had answered the phone. "I think you are going to need to be admitted to the hospital today. I think you were in V tach."

"Okay," I said, finally admitting to myself I had a real problem. A few minutes later, I pulled into the parking lot, using the handicap space. I gingerly got out of the car and walked slowly to the office, my heart feeling like a ticking time bomb. Each step I took was a potential trigger for an explosion. As I walked into the waiting room of the clinic, I was immediately directed to the back where the receptionists and nurses all stared at me in disbelief. I now had all the witnesses I would ever need to testify about the dumbest act I had ever performed in my life.

I was escorted into an exam room where I was immediately processed and set up for admission. Another cardiologist came and discussed the heart catheterization he would need to perform to guarantee I didn't have a lesion in one of my arteries like the YMCA guy's "widow maker." Suddenly, my dream of being "younger next year" seemed to be slipping away. Who cared what I was *next* year? I just wanted to be *older* tomorrow. On this particular day, my focus changed. The proverbial wake-up call had sounded. "I really *do* have a *serious* heart problem," I admitted. "And it is trying to *kill me*."

There were numerous similarities between my physical and spiritual hearts at this time. I hadn't realized how out of control my *spiritual* heart had also become. I wasn't looking at its heart "monitor" to determine the abnormal rhythm it was displaying. What would it take to get my attention? My V tach had surely gotten it. Perhaps in some indirect way, the V tach would get me to pay closer attention to my *other* heart problem too.

The week after I was discharged from the hospital, I gave a long stick to Christine, the nurse who had witnessed my clinic episode on May 5, upon which I had written:

> *This stick is known as the "Christine stick" and can be used at any time by Christine or anyone she endows to beat Dr. Fowler when he illustrates improper or dangerous behavior at the Urgent Care clinics. At no time will she be held responsible for her actions.*

I think she keeps it with her to this day.

Chapter 14

Watch Whose Eyes You Look Into

As a third-year medical student, I learned the importance of knowing when to call for help. It was the first day of my psychiatry rotation on the locked-in inpatient psychiatry floor at the county hospital, where my fellow third-year students and I were standing around awaiting the arrival of the residents and attending physicians. The locked-in psychiatry unit had a creepy feel to it, for none of us had witnessed seriously psychotic or delusional patients before. I remembered stories from other medical students who had previously rotated through the psychiatry service about the bizarre behavior they had witnessed. I didn't know what to expect, but I knew it couldn't be worse than my OB-GYN rotation a few months earlier. *Nothing could be worse than that*, I thought. After our morning conference with the attending and resident physicians, the medical students drew straws to see who would be first to evaluate the next psych patient in the ER. That's right. Lucky me.

Later that morning, the more than slightly overweight unit secretary displayed her dastardly grin to inform me I had a patient who was waiting in the ER. Off I went to dimensions unknown. I rode the old, creaky, cold elevator down to the ER and stepped into the low-ceilinged hallway that was filled with gurneys, medical equipment, and IV poles. With each step I took, I assured myself, "I can handle anything."

In the distance at the end of the claustrophobic hallway, I saw a middle-aged woman on a gurney dressed in an open-in-the-back hospital gown, screaming and moaning. As I approached the nurse's station, the moaning patient caught me in a tractor-beam gaze that many of the psych patients I had heard often possessed. "Never, at any cost," I was warned by my fellow medical students who had previously rotated through the psychiatry service, "allow yourself to get caught in it." Too late. She was reeling me in.

I felt the pull and knew I was doomed, but as I got closer, she turned her gaze away and placed her right hand over her face as if trying to hide. I was relieved to be out of the tractor-beam stare, but it was only for a moment, as she quickly glared back at me. Next, without hesitation and with the most fluid movement only surpassed by a Derek Jeter-throw from shortstop to first base, she removed her upper plate from her mouth and threw it at me with a great heave. I ducked, and the plate flew over me and skidded down the slick-tiled hallway. The charge nurse grabbed the shoulder of my scrubs while I was still crouched on the floor after dodging the airborne teeth and pulled me to my feet. I will never forget her words. "Your first patient is in the padded restraining room with two security guards. The patient on the gurney is your *second* patient."

I cautiously strolled over to the viewing window of the restraining room door, imagining the next scene I might witness. I peeked through the window and saw padded walls surrounding two incredibly weary-eyed security guards who were closely monitoring a patient who looked like Charles Manson's twin and on a bad day. He had long, entangled hair and the wildest pair of eyes I had ever seen. He was pacing frantically back and forth like a caged animal. When he saw me peering into his room, he must have seen the fear on my face, for he immediately leaped toward the window, slammed one side of his face against it, and screamed, "Do you believe in the Lord? Do you believe in the Lord?"

Well, that was it for me. I had reached my maximum capability and hadn't even talked with a patient yet. Like my Chemistry 101 class in college, I was hoping once again that "Superman" would jump from a door somewhere and save the day. No such luck, for unfortunately everything I was witnessing was real, and I had to deal with it head-on. Acknowledging I had more than I could handle, I tucked my tail between my legs and phoned the psychiatry resident to explain, as best I could, the situation in the ER. He must have laughed when thinking of my predicament on my *first* day.

That particular day in the ER, I learned that when faced with a new and extremely difficult situation, I might have to call for help. I also learned the importance of having conditioned reflexes that day, which are essential when dealing with the unknown, for sometimes they can help you from "getting bit" (even by a flying upper plate). If I would have only remembered these lessons when I had V tach at the clinic. Oh, well. Maybe next time.

I was clueless as to the potentially life-threatening consequences of my actions, or perhaps I should say *inactions,* that day in the clinic when I had V tach and blinded to the life-threatening nature of my own problem. I had not dealt with many personal tragedies up to that time in my life. I had primarily managed those of *others*. My true mettle that day was certainly tested. And its weakness clearly expressed.

My blindness wasn't limited to my medical condition alone, for my spiritual sightedness had grown quite dim also. I wasn't capable of reading the images on the spiritual Snellen chart (eye test in a doctor's office) hanging in front of me. I needed a thorough spiritual ophthalmologic exam and a refraction. Now I just needed to figure out how to get to *the* eye doctor's office.

Chapter 15

I Need a New Pair of Specs

The following day after my clinic experience with V tach, I was to have a cardiac catheterization (cath) to make sure I didn't have a blockage in my coronary arteries. Perhaps the stress test I had eleven months prior didn't pick up an arterial plaque, or blockage.

I didn't sleep well the night before, and early that morning around five o'clock, I began thinking about the ensuing procedure. I was fearful for many reasons: My experiences as an emergency medicine physician going to resuscitations in the cath lab to intubate patients while a cardiologist frantically tried to get the patient's heart beating again; being a father and a husband; having a serious heart arrhythmia myself and possibly going into it again *during* the cath; and a weakened faith, causing a lack of assurance as to where I would go if death occurred. I was deeply ashamed of this last thought, but there it was, staring me directly in the face. When it really mattered, I couldn't be sure. What kind of faith did I have? Hadn't I accepted Christ and gained entrance to heaven? Why was I so unsure?

Out of my fear, I wrote the following words to my wife and kids on tear-stained pages:

May 6, 2010

> I understand my problem and the potential for complica-
> tions is very real. As I write this last statement, my eyes
> well up with tears, for no doubt this scares me to think I
> could die during the procedure. Ah, there it is, the word

death. WOW. I've talked about it with patients many times and often had to be the deliverer of such news to anxious family members in the emergency room when their loved one just couldn't make it. I never could grasp their physical pain at that moment when they were given the confirmatory news related to their partner, wife, brother, mother, father, son, daughter, or friend. It is not something I want any of you to go through any time soon. I know God will not give more than any one of us can handle.

I have had up to this point a very wonderful life. I was blessed at the age of seventeen to be given enough faith to respond to the Holy Spirit's tugging of my heart. I am thankful for how my decision to follow Christ has affected every aspect of my entire life from selecting my wife, choosing my career, and raising my children. It also has caused me wonderful anguish at times as I struggled with my aberrant ways, which were inconsistent with Christ's teachings. I watched how I was lead back to His fold and cared for again like a child being held by its mother after getting lost when told before not to stray. I stray at times, but I never forget from where I stray, and over time, as I grow in my faith, the tendency to stray becomes less and less.

Wil, you are gifted with so many things and have a wonderful sensitive heart, which breaks at times and is understanding and caring. Your heart is your strongest strength and enables your other talents to be even greater. You will do very well in life, and I encourage you to seek your passions and dreams while always working toward building your base of knowledge. You can always go through life knowing your father is very proud of you as a man and couldn't be more satisfied as a father!

Morgen. You don't have to be so strong today. You are such a wise, old soul with God-given insights into how people think. Your questions will be answered throughout your life. Don't stop seeking or asking the tough or embarrassing questions. Always seek the truth and know I will always be right behind you every step of the way. Seek an excellent husband. Take care of your mother. I will always love you dearly. I couldn't have asked for a more precious, exquisite daughter.

Cindy, my beloved Cindy. This is too difficult to write, for my vision is blurred from the flow of tears streaming from my eyes. How I have been blessed. Thank you. We will see each other in heaven, but you have much to do here on Earth. This pain will pass, and you will go on. Use your friends, and lean on them now. It's a vulnerable time, but God will protect and nurture you through this. Take care of our wonderful children and know I will always be thinking of you. Your witness for Christ shines always and has provided me such delight while with you. Continue to let it shine even in the midst of hardship, and stay focused as you always do on what really matters. Your love for me is deep, and it has been so much fun being married to you. I can only hope Wil and Morgen have equal opportunities in their futures.

My words resounded with a believer's conviction, yet for some reason, my life didn't reflect the kind of life I thought "a believer's life" should look like. I wondered, "If I know I believe in Christ, why has my life strayed so, and why didn't my belief provide more calm and assurance at such a threatening time?" My perception of my faith was distorted, and as stated earlier, I needed corrective "lenses" in order to "see better." Here I was at the spiritual visual exam and being told my current lenses were weak and my perspective blurry. My spiritual vision should have been refracted years previously, but I had always been satisfied with my myopic view. On this particular morning, just hours before my heart catheterization, I knew I wanted to find a new "pair of specs," but where? I hadn't visited the "optometry shop" for quite some time.

This event was a jolt to my system. I knew it was time to get serious about my health and my faith. I claimed this day as my official starting point to "seeing" more clearly. It may not be easy and it may hurt a little as I search, but I had to find out what was wrong in my life, physically, psychologically, and spiritually. But where would I look? How would I find it? I wasn't totally sure, but I knew where to start, so I prayed fervently that morning, asking God for guidance. I wasn't sure what would happen next or how it would come, but I knew it would occur based on *His* timing, not mine.

The cardiac cath was uneventful and completely normal. *Great*, I thought,

But what was causing my V tach? The following day, the second ablation procedure was performed, but this time, the right ventricle was the site of attack, for my V tach seemed to originate from there. Because of the V tach and its serious threat of death, an ICD (internal cardiac defibrillator)/pacemaker device was inserted into the same site where only a pacemaker had previously occupied. I learned later that evening after my heart's evaluation that my cardiac rhythm had progressed to a third-degree AV heart block as well, the most severe form of AV block, which meant the top of my heart (atria) had no electrical communication with the lower part (ventricles). I was now totally dependent (100 percent) on a dual-chamber pacemaker for *every* beat of my heart. Talk about "being wired for sound," I was now wired for *life*. This was going to take some getting used to.

Chapter 16

A New Roller Coaster

My specialty of emergency medicine demands that I prepare for anything that walks or rolls through the ER doors. I like this orientation to medicine and is the primary reason I switched from OB-GYN to emergency medicine as a specialty. However, some things in life remain too unpredictable and can never be prepared for entirely. When the obscure occurs, you just have to have faith that God will get you through it.

When Cindy and I were newly married, we had saved about five thousand dollars and thought we should do the responsible thing and invest it with a financial consultant. This would be our *first* chance to invest.

I had completed my OB-GYN internship and had become the medical officer of Destroyer Squadron Seven, whose staff was based out of San Diego, California. Cindy was working as a social worker at the Children's Hospital in San Diego. We had purchased a small bungalow-style house in the quaint inner city community of San Diego called Hillcrest. We enjoyed the urban life and all its associated pleasantries.

We had finally gotten ahead financially, and being the children of Depression-era parents, we knew it was never too early to start saving. We both were novices in the world of finance, so we arranged a meeting with a financial advisor who introduced us to our new and exciting investment strategy. Our consultant seemed knowledgeable and trustworthy, so we gave him a twenty-five hundred dollar check, which he gladly accepted and placed in his zippered pouch. The next day, he contacted us and told us he had bought some mutual funds. "Wow, we are all grown up now!" Cindy and I thought. We owned a house and now were investing. "My dad would be proud," I reflected. The financial advisor had placed the purchase on a *Friday*. Who knew how much richer we would be by Monday?

Anyone who invests has heard of a special Monday in October 1987 called "Black Monday." This day is known for having the largest percentage point drop in stock market history when the Dow plunged 507.99 points, or 22.6 percent, in *one* day. "These things happen in the market," I guessed. But now it was happening to *my* money! Money I had invested the *DAY BEFORE*. What were the odds of this happening one business day after our first attempt at investing our hard-earned money? It scared the living daylights out of Cindy and me as we watched nearly half of our twenty-five hundred dollars go bye-bye in *one* day.

A seasoned trader might think of this day as a great moment to purchase more stock at a bargain price, but to the novice investor like me, it was a time to put my tail between my legs and run. So as any normal person would react, I sold and got out of there while I still had something to get out with.

"Oh well, live and learn," I decided. Unfortunately, this event caused us to not invest for a significant period of time and we missed substantial investment opportunities, for the Dow Industrial average increased 72 percent in the following four years. My financial whiplash was severe, recovery took awhile, and the consequences were great.

These first events and my responses to them had a costly (in more than just dollars) influence on my life. The financial experience was equitable to riding a roller coaster with no crossbar, blindfolded, and not knowing when the next turn would occur. My spiritual life felt similar. How could I find a safer way to ride through the sharp turns and downhill spirals of life? I wanted to enjoy the scary turns without fearing I would leave the tracks. I needed to find a new roller coaster ride I could trust and enjoy.

Chapter 17

I'm Asking, Seeking, and Knocking

I enjoy preparing for medical and traumatic emergencies, but the arrival of my own heart emergency through the sliding doors of an ER where I didn't work was a situation I could never have prepared for. I felt like a third-year medical student all over again having no control and feeling lost like I did that first day on the psychiatry service when the lady threw her teeth at me. Any spiritual or psychological preparation for managing my heart condition's complications or dealing with its stresses should have taken place long before now, but my life and its daily disciplines hadn't prepared me for what was ahead. I was at the mercy of cardiologists to diagnose and treat my cardiac enigma and was completely dependent on not two, but now three wires connected to a pacemaker and a device known as an ICD, which I am told will kick me in the chest like a jackass if it ever goes off. How could I have prepared myself for anything like that?

My thoughts during this time were concentrated on the physical since those issues were blatantly staring me in the face, but spiritual issues were beginning to enter my thoughts too. Soon after my hospitalization, I began reading *Fearless* by Max Lucado, who happens to be my pastor at Oak Hills Church in San Antonio. His books are down-to-earth, much like his West Texas upbringing. They are quite poignant, enjoyable, and enlightening, and as I began my journey to discover my own fears, I appreciated his kind and insightful thoughts based on the Word of God, or the Bible.

I participated in a Bible study that summer with some good friends and a few others I didn't know. We reviewed a book along with its teaching video called *The Prodigal God: Recovering the Heart of the Christian Faith* by Dr. Tim

Keller. Its discussion detailed the story of the prodigal son as told in Luke 15:11–32. Dr. Keller, whose writings I have come to love, is inspirational, and his book and video provided a format for me to discuss my questions and thoughts I was struggling with related to my faith with friends. I remember stating to the other men at the beginning of the Bible study, "I'm not sure why you are here, but I have a serious medical problem and want to know what God is going to show me about my faith through this study." No doubt, I was on a mission and hoped God would guide me on a path of righteousness. Certainly a book that had *Recovering the Heart of the Christian Faith* as a subtitle should help me find what I was searching for, right?

I read a third book that summer called *Counterfeit Gods*, also by Dr. Keller, which discusses the many idols we can have in our lives and how to recognize them and avoid worshipping them. This story was not far from the teachings of Jeremiah to the Jews related to their errant ways worshipping gods ("worthless idols") separate from the God of Abraham who had delivered them from bondage in Egypt years before while being led by Moses. Dr. Keller's teachings are very attentive to psychological issues of the Christian, which I appreciated greatly during this trying time.

The following summer months were associated with a renewed interest in learning *why* I believed what I did and *why* I was fearful that day in the hospital when faced with the possibility of dying. Why was I unsure, and why did I doubt? In the past, I had missed great opportunities to grow my faith when times were tough because I turned away from His leading and teaching. Not this time! I wanted to dive into the Word, read books about it, and listen to music and sermons related to it. I needed to know where I stood, and I wasn't going to be the reason this time for not growing. I knew God wanted me to grow, too, for He promises that if I ask, He will give, if I seek, I shall find, and if I knock, He will open the door (Matthew 7:7).

As my illness progressively worsened through July and August, I started to develop V tach episodes during any stressful activity. One hot day while sitting at my son's baseball game, I saw him get hit in the chest by a hard-hit line drive while he was pitching. It knocked his breath out, but miraculously he was able to get to the ball and, from his knees, throw the batter out at first as the third-base runner was running home with two outs. It was an incredible play, but afterward I became extremely concerned when he collapsed to the ground.

Since I was an ER doc (and a concerned parent), I went immediately onto the field to check his status. After a few minutes, he was able to catch his breath and walk back to the dugout. I exited the field with my usual calm ER physician persona, but inside, I was pretty distraught. My epinephrine (adrenaline) was pumping full blast, which caused my heart to go haywire and into V tach. I had to lay flat for ten minutes on a bleacher seat to prevent myself from passing out. Cindy calculated her next move in case I became unconscious. All the parents around me thought I was just kicking back and resting with my cap over my face. They never knew how close they were to starting CPR. Cindy was about to call an ambulance seconds before my chest went "thud" and started beating regularly again. I finally was able to sit up without feeling like I was going to pass out. I exited the park when the game ended, looking like an arthritic old man cradling his heart, hoping not to disturb the abominable rhythm monster lurking inside. After that episode, I didn't sit in the bleachers for the rest of the summer but in my air-conditioned Suburban where I could watch over the right field fence.

Any event that stressed my system seemed to put me into V tach. Even taking a hot shower became too much. Exerting myself became severely limited. I rarely went outdoors apart from doctor visits because of the summer heat. Climbing the one staircase at home now took me ten minutes to reach the top. The progression of my heart's problem with no etiology caused my EP cardiologist to recommend I visit another type of cardiology specialist who primarily worked with transplant cardiac patients. This was certainly another wake-up call. I felt the proverbial clock ticking faster and faster!

The transplant cardiologist was a very bright, pleasant guy who discussed my problem in great detail. He understood my dire straits and explained, "I want to perform biopsies of the inside of your heart to see if I can determine the etiology of your problem." I was ready for anything at this point and hung onto his every word, for I was a man who was desperately searching for answers. It was a Thursday, and he said I would be admitted the following Monday.

"Perhaps, I will finally get a diagnosis," I hoped. Maybe he could find that yet undetectable clue and provide my physicians the opportunity to diagnose and treat. As I walked out of his office that hot August afternoon, I felt positive that this could possibly be the procedure that would solve my medical riddle once and for all.

I got into my car and drove away, feeling better and more hopeful than I had for quite some time. Now I just needed to make it to Monday.

Chapter 18

The Big Bang

Have you ever witnessed a moment in history that became forever etched in your mind? Like Neil Armstrong landing on the moon, Kennedy's assassination, 9/11, or the moment you heard your mother or father had died? Those moments become so poignant and memorable.

One of those moments was about to happen to me. After my office visit with the transplant cardiologist, I stopped by a Borders bookstore to purchase a book for a friend who recently had a cardiac bypass. Leaving the store, I noticed a Chipotle restaurant down the street. I was hungry, so I drove to the restaurant to catch a bite. I parked in front of the restaurant. As I got out of the car, the hot Texas sun blasted me like a coal-burning furnace. Feeling quite lightheaded, I immediately sat down, thinking I was having one of my episodes. Sweating and noticing that my heart was beating irregularly, I closed the door and turned the air conditioner to full blast. Still not feeling well and noting I was about to pass out, I reclined my seat back to lay flat.

BANG!

"What just happened?" I questioned through my mental fog. It was as if everyone outside was moving in slow motion, and I hadn't a clue why. I recounted the events leading up to this moment, and it finally hit me. "Oh my God, my defibrillator went off!" I couldn't believe it. I checked my pulse; it was beating regularly at around eighty beats a minute. While regaining my senses, I remembered when it felt like an eighteen-wheeler had hit the rear end of my car. I started to chuckle, realizing I had been shocked by my ICD, thinking that if it hadn't done its job, I would be dead right now. I didn't know if I had transiently passed out or not, but I knew I didn't want it to happen again. *I now know how hard a jackass kicks*, I thought while thinking about others who had described their being shocked by their ICD.

A few minutes later, after realizing there were no Chipotles in heaven, I called Cindy. I told her what had happened, and that I would sit for a while and then drive home. She wasn't going to let me drive this time after having V tach, especially after being defibrillated, so she told me to stay put, and that she was on her way.

After I hung up, I called an old friend who has an ICD and told him what had happened. He said, "You don't sound too good" and requested I call my cardiologist. I agreed and then phoned my EP cardiologist. I finally believed I didn't "sound too good" when the *receptionist* asked me to call 911. She didn't even patch me through to the doctor. I am thankful for her courage to tell me what to do.

I turned on my car's caution lights so EMS would recognize my car. While waiting for the ambulance, Cindy drove up, opened the passenger door, and sat in the seat next to me. Seeing the fear on her face, I tried to downplay the moment, but it was no use. I was not doing well, and she knew it.

An ambulance arrived, and my door opened. It was a paramedic I had known for many years while working in the ERs of San Antonio. He was as surprised to see me as I was to see him, but I was sure glad he was there. He and his partner carefully loaded me onto a gurney after moving me slowly from the car, hoping to not excite my heart too much and cause it to go into a bad rhythm again. Off we went to the ER. I had one more episode of V tach during the transport, but the antitachycardic pacing (ATP) component of the ICD caught it on the third try and slowed the V tach down. If it doesn't work the third time, the ICD defibrillates and shocks me.

I am so thankful for the ATP function of the ICD. I have observed patients who were shocked over and over again by their ICD, and it is not a pretty site. Those patients are severely traumatized from the repeated violence. I had been traumatized enough for one day. I didn't want any more.

The transplant cardiologist I had met two hours earlier came to the ER. He greeted me with a cautious smile and said, "If you wanted to be admitted to the hospital *this* bad, you could have just told me when you were in the clinic." I laughed and then thought about the timing of this episode and how I had no control over my life these days.

Chapter 19

No Control—Again

I was deployed to the Indian Ocean as the medical officer of Destroyer Squadron Seven in the fall of 1987. Our squadron was part of a battle group in the Gulf of Oman, which included the USS *Missouri* (battleship), USS *Ranger* (aircraft carrier), USS *Long Beach* (nuclear cruiser), and surrounding support ships, including oilers, supply ships, destroyers, and frigates. This was my first WESTPAC, or six-month deployment, to the western Pacific Ocean and beyond. Our mission was to destroy offshore oilrigs, which belonged to Iran in the Persian Gulf in retaliation for what I thought was the bombing of the USS *Stark* on May 17, 1987, in Yemen. I discovered later that Iraq had hit the *Stark*. Who knows?

I had never been surrounded for so many consecutive days by that much water in my life. After being out to sea for forty-four days straight, I had developed sea legs for the first time and was getting stir crazy from cabin fever. I thought I had reached the end of my capacity to tolerate one more day at sea when my boss, the commodore, asked (ordered) me to go down to a tiny island known as Diego Garcia to board another ship, the USS *Holt* out of Hawaii, that would be steaming to Mauritius, Seychelles, and then to India. I couldn't believe it. A reprieve. I wasn't going to hesitate to take that job, but it dawned on me that I didn't know how I was going to get there. But I would worry about that later, for right then, I knew I was going to a place where I could plant my feet on dry land, and I was willing to put up with any mode of transportation to do that.

Diego Garcia is a tiny little island on the southern side of the equator in the Indian Ocean that looks like a dot on a globe. I knew it had a telephone to call home and an Officer's, or "O," Club where I could relax without the constant pitching and rolling I had grown accustomed to on the ships. I also would be able to down a few very well-deserved, icy cold beers.

The ship I was to board was docked there already, so I had to fly down to meet it. During my WESTPAC, I had taken off from the flight deck of the carrier many times and always by helicopter. The other ships in the battle group didn't have a physician aboard, and since they were located relatively close to the carrier, a helicopter was the perfect vehicle to transport me the short distance when I needed to visit for medical reasons. But I knew one of those vertically oriented flying machines wasn't going to take me to Diego Garcia, for it was much, much farther away than the support ships. This meant only one thing—*a jet catapult launch.* This would be my first.

I packed my bags for a long stay since the USS *Holt* would be separated from the battle group for a few weeks. My jet was a carrier-based, subsonic, all-weather, long-range, electronic reconnaissance (ELINT) aircraft known as an S3A and was already being prepped for takeoff on the USS *Ranger*'s flight deck runway.

I exited the bridge tower and entered the jet through a hatch on the underbelly of the plane. After the hatch was slammed shut and latched, I literally sat on the hatch, which I hoped had been locked securely. I really didn't want to be dropped into the Indian Ocean from a cruising altitude thousands of feet above the planet.

I was positioned a couple of feet behind the two pilots and could see the instruments and windshield quite well. *This is just like Top Gun!* I thought while anxiously awaiting the "cleared for takeoff" from the tower. *Top Gun*'s red-carpet premier was the previous year in San Diego where Cindy and I lived, so it was still fresh in my mind. But now I wasn't just watching it on the theater screen. I was living it!

All the flight deck crew members, dressed in various colored shirts that designated their specific jobs, were scurrying about and readying the deck for takeoff. The "plane director," or the guy who bends down, points his hands forward, and gives the pilot the go-ahead to takeoff, was watching everyone. I could hear *Danger Zone* by Kenny Loggins echoing in my ears. *This is going to be fun!* I thought as I prepared for takeoff.

Immediately after the go-ahead from the plane director, the pilot saluted, the jet accelerated, and it felt as if every square millimeter of skin on my face was being ripped off. A few seconds later, a release occurred, and we were flying, but it seemed more like floating. A slight tilt to the right, and all I could see was water. *We are going to crash!* I panicked, but the skilled navy pilots slowly turned the jet and up and away we flew. I couldn't believe anyone could control an aircraft with such a significant force, but that was what these guys were trained for. And they were definitely trained well.

After an hour into the flight, the pilots seemed concerned about an instrument reading of which I could not discern. They took the jet out of autopilot and tapped on the instrument panel. Then they did something quite unnerving. They moved or "jostled" the jet with a gyroscopic action, which felt as if the whole jet was going out of control. The pilots looked at their gauges, gave the okay sign to each other, and returned to autopilot.

This series of maneuvers recurred two more times, and after the third time, the pilots thought it would be nice to tell the doc in the back what was going on. I was thankful they acknowledged my presence. What they told me, though, didn't comfort me at all, and I wished they had kept quiet. They calmly explained that the fuel in one wing needed to be moved over to the other wing since it was not transferring on its own. *Okay, let's get this jet to Diego Garcia right now!* I silently pleaded within my mind. However, the pilots never seemed too worried, and I took great comfort in their calmness the rest of the trip—but only after I had settled down from the initial shock.

I had *no control* over this flight or its destiny. I was at the mercy of the jet, the pilots, and thousands of feet of air over a vast ocean below. I had to learn to sit back and enjoy the ride, for there was *nothing* I was able to do to make the flight any safer.

I learned to have greater confidence in professionals who are doing their jobs after that flight to Diego Garcia, and I continued to have that same confidence as I entered the cath lab where the transplant cardiologist would perform five endocardial (inside lining of the heart) biopsies the day after my being shocked by my ICD. I noticed it wasn't *just* the professionals I was confident in that day, though, for I was beginning to recognize God's control over what was happening, too.

I knew I had received a wake-up call on May 5, 2010, the day of my initial V tach episode at my clinic. Since then, I had diligently sought answers to my many questions, as my illness was progressing, and I realized I had a more significant problem than everyone had originally thought.

As I prayed and studied my texts along with my Bible that summer, I discovered I had an even *deeper* problem with my *spiritual* heart. More detailed probing was needed, and I was willing to go wherever needed to find the answers. My life was on the line. I needed answers, but more importantly, I needed assurance.

Chapter 20

A New Life

My life took a 180-degree turn after the literally shocking event in front of Chipotle. The frequency of V tach episodes was increasing and their associated rates, or beats per minute (bpm), were increasing too. These factors made for more symptomatic episodes. Never in a million years did I ever think I would be able to say, "My V tach was worsening," but here I was, dealing with it daily.

All my biopsies came back normal. "How could this be?" I wondered, expecting that this would be the moment of clarity for my illness. Dejected and worn out, I returned home from the hospital. But I was returning to a new world.

After my hospitalization and since I had been defibrillated, I wasn't allowed to work in the clinics, as it was too stressful for me and too dangerous for my patients. I couldn't drive and always had to have someone with me in the pool in case my ICD went off, for I might drown. Ladders, forget it. I had never felt so helpless and dependent in all my life. Maybe there was something to learn from this dependent lifestyle. Perhaps I was supposed to depend on something *far greater*. I didn't know it at the time, but God was revealing to me my many idols and how dependent I was on them for success, satisfaction, and confidence. He began showing me that He wanted to be the only thing I depended on and worshipped. Period!

There I was, sitting around the house with more time on my hands than I thought I would ever have. I was always walking on eggshells, for the irregularity in my heartbeats occurred regularly. I continued having V tach episodes, and my ability to do anything about them was diminishing.

Although I was taking medications, they weren't stopping the progression of the illness. I never knew or could predict when I would feel weak or faint. Sometimes it would last for an hour, other times seconds to minutes. When I did venture out of the house, episodes occurred at restaurants and once at "Meet the Teachers" night at my son's high school. Later, my wife and many of my patients told me they were quite worried at that event because I didn't look well. I wasn't able to keep up with other parents after the bell rang as they rushed to the next classroom that coincided with their child's class schedule. I finally gave up, played hookie, and sat at a picnic table until Cindy was finished visiting with Wil's teachers.

The waitresses at Bear Moon also noticed I wasn't looking well. I was frail and my color was deteriorating. Looking back, I am surprised by how accustomed I had gotten going into and out of V tach. I could tell by the stares of others that while I didn't see the full impact of my illness upon me, they did.

During those long days sitting around the house, I began journaling. I knew it could provide healing during trial and hardship, and it also had been recommended to me by a physician friend who had used this technique while dealing with her battle with cancer. I am so thankful for her recommendation.

Journaling is like sitting on a psychiatrist's couch, sharing your deepest thoughts and fears. When the content of the conversation is directed heavenward, the psychiatrist takes on a whole new appearance, and His medical degree originates from the most prestigious institution in the universe. I knew chronic stressful illnesses could affect one's psyche, and I needed to help myself as much as possible, but I had no idea how helpful journaling would be and what it would reveal. Frequently, I penned my thoughts, concerns, memories, and discoveries while traveling along my newfound path, documenting each bend in the road. My many thoughts needed filtering through a sieve I could trust, for I desperately wanted to make sense of all this mess.

I am thankful I serve a God of order who doesn't want me to be confused or to wander aimlessly. He desires my attention and presence. He doesn't want me to be lost and is patient as He leads me ever so gently back.

So here I was, sitting around the house all day with nothing to do. "Hey, God. Let's have a conversation."

The Conversation

I. Preparing My Heart

Chapter 21

The Conversation Begins

On August 26, I began a conversation with God related to the most intense and revealing segment of my journey. I had no idea where I was being led, but I trusted Him. I documented prayers, thoughts, book passages and influential Bible verses I experienced along the way chronologically with passion, tears, and growing insight related to my hearts' illnesses. These journal entries gradually revealed a bigger picture that God wanted me to understand. I am confident of His presence during this time and assured of His desire for me to draw closer to Him. I will forever treasure these pages and the precious memories and insights they contain.

I was ready to be molded. The clay was soft, the potter's wheel was spinning, and I was ready for His gentle touch.

Journal Entries
(Journal entries are noted in the font shown here.)

August 26, 2010

> *"... For out of the overflow of his heart his mouth speaks" (Luke 6:45).*

*I read an editorial by columnist David Brooks entitled **A Case of Mental Courage** describing the loss of "mental character" in our country* and how "*very few in public life habitually step back and think about the weakness in their own thinking and what they should do to compensate.*" (**New York Times**, *August 23, 2010*) *The article begins with a story about "the popular novelist Fanny Burney" who lived in the early 1800s. In 1811, she was diagnosed with breast cancer and later recounted her experience of having a mastectomy* **without** *anesthesia. Brooks noted her "ability to face unpleasant thoughts" as an act of mental heroism. I have had plenty of unpleasant thoughts the last few months. How will I face them? What will my "mental heroism" look like? Brooks noted that Burney "lived at a time when people were more conscious of the fallen nature of men and women. People were held to be* **inherently sinful**, *and to be a decent person one had to* **struggle against one's** *weakness" (emphases mine).*

What are my weaknesses? What am I struggling with in order to help me be a more "decent person"? I am searching, but answers are not forthcoming. I know one thing, though; I have been quite fearful since May 5, and my problems seem to be increasing. What if no one can find out what is causing me to progress so methodically from simple, asymptomatic atrial rhythm problems to life-threatening ventricular rhythms that seem to have a mind of their own and are now associated with third-degree AV heart block that allows **no communication** *between my heart's upper and lower chambers?*

> *Out of you (Bethlehem) will come for me one who will be ruler over Israel, whose origins are from of old, from ancient times. (Micah 5:2)*
>
> *Required of You? ...* **Act justly, love mercy**, *and* **walk humbly** *with your God! (Micah 6:8, emphasis added)*
>
> *God saw how they (Nineveh) turned from their evil ways. He had compassion and did not bring upon them the destruction he had threatened. (Jonah 3:10)*

Grace and mercy. My understanding of these two terms is this. **Grace** *is receiving from God a gift I do not deserve and haven't earned.* **Mercy** *is God withholding His wrath I so rightly deserve. These verses started me thinking more about these two topics. I also am trying to figure out their meanings in my life. Sure, I know I have received God's grace through the gift of Jesus Christ, but why don't I* **feel** *His grace? I certainly am not feeling His mercy!*

August 27, 2010

> *Do not fear those who kill the body and after that can do no more. Fear Him who, after the killing of the body, has power to throw you into hell. Yes, I tell you, fear Him ... Indeed, the very hairs of your head are all numbered. Don't be afraid; you are worth more than many sparrows. (Luke 12:4–5, 7)*

August 29, 2010

> *I conquered a worthless idol today. A small step, but thank You, Lord. Help me to know how to love You today with all my heart, soul, strength, and mind.*

> *Who is my neighbor today?*

August 30, 2010

> *"For where your treasure is, there your **heart** will be also" (Luke 12:34, emphasis added).*

My readings and thoughts for months have centered on the condition of my physical heart, but this week I began to seriously look at my spiritual heart and its condition. My spiritual heart is diseased and needs significant resuscitation, for its care has been compromised over the years. It continues to beat, but not vibrantly, and it isn't performing at its greatest potential. God wants me to have a spirit-filled heart, performing at maximal efficiency and pumping a joyful flow from its chambers with each beat. I am hindering that flow through my lack of seeking Him and His will for me. My heart is in the repair shop, as layers of dirt and grime are slowly being pulled away and its true status revealed. It is an ugly site, but oh, how good it is to see the dirt and grime being stripped away. I can't do it myself. I don't own the mechanic's shop.

*My V tach episodes are occurring with greater frequency, and at my follow-up visit with the EP cardiologist, I asked, "Is it time for me to consider going somewhere else to **find an answer**?" He agreed, and of all places, Cleveland, Ohio, is my destination. I have heard a lot of "Cleveland" jokes in the past, but Cleveland apparently has an outstanding cardiovascular facility named the Cleveland Clinic that no* *one can joke about. It probably is the best cardiac care center in the world. My cardiologist contacted them, discussed my case, and then set up a telephone conversation between their electrophysiology (cardiology) department and me. I will always appreciate my San Antonio EP cardiologist's humility for starting this process for me.*

Cindy, friends, family, prior patients of mine, and I later learned that even church members from outside my local community whom I had never met were all praying for my recovery and healing. No doubt many were also praying for my spiritual recovery, for both heart conditions were in severe trouble, and the wise knew which to pray for. I will always be extremely thankful for their prayers, and I know that God is aware of each kind act.

Chapter 22

What Have I Caused?

My third and final baby-related "first" story illustrates the origin of some of my bewilderment regarding my life and relationship to God. This particular event caused Cindy and I much anguish and nailed what seemed at the time to be the final spike into a heart that was struggling to hang onto its first love.

Cindy and I married in 1985 and moved to San Diego, where we lived for six years, after I graduated from medical school. The first year was my internship in OB-GYN. The next two years, I served on Destroyer Squadron Seven's staff, and the last three I spent at the Balboa Naval Hospital training in emergency medicine. When I was a third-year emergency medicine resident at Balboa in 1990, Cindy and I had been trying to get pregnant for a year and were starting to wonder if something was wrong.

One day, Cindy came home beaming and said, "I'm pregnant!" Finally, we were pregnant. Cindy's dream had come true. She had dreamed of being a mom since she was a little girl. Her passion for being a mom preceded my passion to be a doctor by years. She has a sweet spirit and had a passion for Christ, which I have envied, especially during years of struggle. Cindy knew I had a good heart, but she also knew I wasn't doing much to strengthen my relationship with God or to grow spiritually. But she remained patient and persevered. My hope is that for the rest of her life Cindy knows her husband loves her dearly and serves the same Savior she does with passion and commitment.

While pregnant, Cindy was working a stressful job as a Licensed Clinical Social Worker (LCSW) on a cardiovascular unit at the children's hospital in San Diego. She was good at it, too; however, it was difficult with the occasional death of a child who didn't make it after surgery. Cindy dealt with grief-stricken parents, trying to console and help them during probably the most difficult time of their lives. It takes a special gift to do this type of work.

While at work one afternoon, Cindy called me and said she was having "some bleeding." She was in her eleventh week of pregnancy and was scared. After having attended to hundreds of women in the ER with similar symptoms, I knew that the outcome might not be good. The probability of a miscarriage in the United States is 14–28 percent, depending on the age of the mother (a higher rate as the mother's age increases). Regardless of statistics, though, it is a 100 percent probability for the mother who is going through this awful drama.

We met with a physician in the OB-GYN department who was an old friend since my internship. After an ultrasound and lab tests, it looked like our greatest fear was happening before our eyes. Tears of sorrow came, and I tried to console Cindy the best I could, reminding her that one miscarriage has no influence on future pregnancies. She knew I was trying to help, but what she needed at this time was God and a man who would lead her to Him with encouragement and comforting words. But I was not that man.

I was lost. Those old fearful feelings of never being forgiven for past sins haunted me once again. Incredible! The first pregnancy with my wife, a godly woman who deserved a beautiful child, was having it taken away. I knew Cindy would be the perfect mom. So many pregnancies end up this way, but *why her*? Why us? Why this "first" time? I was angry and felt deeper guilt than ever before. Had my sin caused my wife this torment? "Dear God, let it not be so," I pleaded.

My spiritual life went into a tailspin that seemed endless. How many times would I be reminded of past sins? Why did I still languish because of them? Did I feel I still had a chance with God? If so, what did I need to do? Where do I turn? Truthful answers can hurt, but they also can be freeing. In John 8:32, Jesus states, "You will know the truth, and the truth will set you free" when speaking to the Jewish believers who "held to His teaching."

Did I hold to His teaching? Did I know the truth? Why didn't I feel like I was set free? I thought I knew the truth, which I did, but the real problem I faced was I didn't feel the truth was known *about me*. To whom did I need to tell? I thought I had confessed to God many times, but it never seemed enough. Why would I not allow myself to be forgiven? Did I understand Christ and His purpose? Why was there a roadblock?

God reveals answers in His own time and at His own pace, and why He takes longer with some I cannot explain. My journey was starting to reveal many important questions. I would be patient while waiting for the answers.

Chapter 23

Okay, Let's Do It Your Way

August 30, 2010 (evening)

While reading Tim Keller's book, *Counterfeit Gods*, I asked,

> *"What idols have I created from the dust of this world that separate me from discovering my heart's deepest desire?"*

1. ***My comfort:*** *Having comfort helps me to avoid reminders of the consequences of man's fallen nature/original sin. Ms. Burney, who had discussed her experience with an anesthetic-free mastectomy, certainly understood discomfort and had no problem with this idol.*

2. ***My success:*** *Conquering others provides me a sense of superiority over them.*

3. ***Protection*** *from people knowing my sinfulness: Do I hold other people's opinion of me higher than God's opinion of me?*

4. ***Security:*** *My own protection from this turbulent world: wealth, position, job, and status.*

5. ***Avoiding physical pain:*** *Afraid of a bodily symptom more than my spiritual well-being. How did Christ suffer?*

6. ***Notoriety:*** *Pumped up by other people, not by God.*

These are some of the worthless idols I have clung to for far too long.

"Those who cling to worthless idols forfeit the grace that could be theirs" (Jonah 2:8).

I can cling to them no longer. The lies and deceit I fooled myself with over the years have hindered and forfeited the grace I long for. My fearfulness needs to turn toward God, Christ, and the Holy Spirit. I need to learn to love with all my heart, soul, strength, and mind and to share that love with my neighbor.

August 31, 2010

Yesterday, an EP cardiologist from the Cleveland Clinic called me at my home. I was very surprised to find out he was the head of the department of electrophysiology at the Cleveland Clinic. We discussed my illness, and he obtained a basic history over the phone. He was soft-spoken but direct with his questions. He explained he had seventeen electrophysiologists in his department and thought there were six available to manage my case. I explained to him I was a Christian, and that the doctor I ultimately ended up with would be in God's hands. He understood. He said he would like to manage my case, but his schedule was too full, so he couldn't see me for at least three months. I told him I understood and would be glad to have any of the physicians he recommended.

At this time, my San Antonio doctors suspected what my diagnosis might be, but until they could get a tissue (biopsy) diagnosis, they weren't going to treat me with the medication they thought I might need. I understood their predicament, but this was *my* life, *my* heart, and I wasn't getting any better. Actually, I was getting worse. I didn't care which cardiologist in Cleveland saw me as long as we could get a diagnosis and start treating my problem. "I'm getting desperate here!" I said under my breath.

I read the story about Naaman (2 Kings 5), who was commander of the army of the king of Aram. He was a powerful man, but he had a little problem. He suffered from leprosy. His Jewish servant girl told him of a man in Samaria who could cure him of his ailment, so Naaman asked permission from his king to go to Israel. His king blessed the trip and sent a letter to the king of Israel, notifying him of Naaman's intentions and his desire for the king of Israel to cure his servant. Naaman left with significant amounts of gold, silver, and clothing for the king of Israel. However, the king of Israel was irate after reading the letter. He thought the king of Aram wanted to pick a fight with him, for the king of Israel knew there was no way he could cure the man of his leprosy.

*The prophet Elisha heard of the situation and told the king of Israel to send the man to him. Naaman finally went to the humble dwelling where Elisha lived. Elisha was the man the Jewish servant girl had told Naaman about. After knocking at Elisha's door, Naaman was told by Elisha's assistants to wash himself in the river Jordan seven times and his illness would be cured. Now Naaman was a very important man (at least in his own mind) and wanted to be treated with respect. He wanted Elisha to come out and show him the respect he **deserved**. Certainly his disease and status warranted more than this! There should be waving of the prophet's hands, etc. Nope, he was given basic instructions from Elisha's assistants to go wash in the Jordan River. Naaman, humiliated, walked away from the house, enraged. Later, his servants convinced him to take the prophet's advice. He finally conceded and went to the Jordan and dipped himself into the river seven times. He was completely healed.*

My hope is that I will find healing, and that it will be on God's terms and with His grace. I do not want to receive care based on how I think I should be treated. My hope of a cure remains strong, and I know any control I think I have over this process is waning. I am beginning to let go. I will follow your lead, Lord.

However, do not rejoice that the spirits submit to you, but rejoice that your names are written in heaven. (Luke 10:20)

So, because you are lukewarm—neither hot nor cold—I am about to spit you out of my mouth. (Revelation 3:16)

I truly wanted my name to be written in heaven, but I questioned my faith and God's reaction to it. I desperately needed reassurance that God was still part of my life. This issue of assurance was the root of much of my fear leading up to this point. I sought His answer daily and would be patient for His response.

Chapter 24

Remember Me

September 9, 2010

> *My prayer today is that I will remain persistent in my quest for God and seek Him as earnestly in good health as in bad. I will not settle any longer to serve/seek Him **as needed,** but to seek Him **always.** His perspective is that I need Him every second of every day and night, in good health and in bad.*

> *"For everyone who exalts himself will be humbled, and he who humbles himself will be exalted" (Luke 18:14).*

September 10, 2010

> *We are unworthy servants; we have only done our duty. (Luke 17:10)*

> *The kingdom of God does not come with your careful observation, nor will people say, "Here it is," or "There it is," because the kingdom of God is within (among) you. (Luke 17:20)*

> *He will be handed over to the Gentiles. They will mock him, insult him, spit on him, flog him, and kill him. (Luke 18:32)*

We live in the kingdom of God while on this earth, for He created it. He does dwell amongst us. It isn't God's time physically to be here as when Christ was with us or when God partially revealed Himself in the Old Testament to Moses, but His Holy Spirit is here now as He lives in our hearts. God is with us, living out His miracles, testimony, and expressions of goodness through the individuals whose hearts He has touched. If Christ lives in me, He can walk with anyone whom I am in contact today. Do I see myself as God's vehicle on this earth? Can He, given my current state of mind, strength, heart, and soul? Individual lives illustrate God's love in this era since Christ ascended. Do I know the privilege I have been given? Why do I put up roadblocks to God expressing His love through me? I am not Christ, and my thinking doesn't confuse me, but I can be more like Christ if I allow my body, soul, and mind to be vulnerable to His love, teaching, and discipline. May any good thing I do glorify God, and may I be content to be His servant. I look forward with rejoicing to seeing my name written in heaven.

September 13, 2010

"Everyone who falls on that stone will be broken to pieces, but he on whom it falls will be crushed" (Luke 20:18; reference to Psalm 118:22, "The stone the builders rejected has become the capstone").

I'd rather be "broken to pieces" rather than crushed by the capstone (Christ). Lord, help me to fall upon the rock. Thank You for Your mercy.

*"He is not the God of the dead, but of the living, for to Him **all are alive**" (Luke 20:38, emphasis added).*

When Jesus spoke of "this age," in Luke 18:30 and Luke 20:34, He was referring to people on this earth. Do I see myself as ageless? How much do I do for all the ages each day? Which age do I seek to serve? How do my actions serve all the ages? Am I only content with what this age provides? How do I limit my nearsightedness? Oh Lord, help me to see beyond this age and let it affect my understanding, thinking, and actions toward and in honor of You only.

September 14, 2010

"This poor widow has put in more than all the others" (Luke 21:3).

"All these people gave their gifts out of their wealth, but she out of her poverty put in all she had" (Luke 21:4).

*Is my wealth hindering me from growing in Christ? How do I give? What sacrifices do I need to make? What do I really need? Am I afraid of letting God have control of my finances? My life? Who benefits from my spending? How do I give out of **my poverty**?*
I reviewed the areas of poverty in my life: time, health, faith, and discipline. If I could give amply from these areas, taking care of any wealth will follow.

September 15, 2010

"The spirit gives life; the flesh counts for nothing. The words are spirit and life" (John 6:63).

"When their spirit departs, they return to the ground" (Psalm 146:3-4).

September 18, 2010

In Luke 23, the responsibility for the "death penalty" does not lie with the Romans, Pilate, or Herod, but with the people. Pilate and Herod announce there is nothing this man has done to deserve death.

*"Christ died for all the people [**all of us**] who have yelled out with our sinful lives 'kill Him'" (Luke 23:15).*

Lord, have mercy on me.

September 19, 2010

"I tell you the truth; today you will be with me in Paradise" (Luke 23:43, One of the most beautiful verses in the Bible to me).

My conviction related to my sinful life and its impact on Christ's suffering is becoming more and more clear. The criminal hanging next to Jesus at His crucifixion wasn't thinking of himself when talking to the other criminal who was mocking Christ. He said, "Don't you fear

God? You are under the same sentence (death)?" All he could say to Jesus was "Remember me." His faith allowed him to spend eternity with Christ in paradise.

My sentence is the same as everyone's: death. I do not desire to go to hell. I choose instead to fear God and say, "Remember me." Christ, You died on the cross, and You did nothing wrong!

Chapter 25

Just Potholes, Not Roadblocks

September 19, 2010 (evening)

I drew this picture years ago to describe a Christian's journey and have shared my interpretation with my kids. I'm sure there is a similar illustration already, but this is my rendition.

My illustration of a Christian's path.

The picture depicts a pair of hands on a handlebar guiding a bicycle along a curbed pathway filled with potholes and lined by gnarly, thorny Texas mesquite trees which lead to a distant cross.

The path corresponds to God's will for the Christian's life that everyone, if desired, can travel. The bicycle symbolizes each person's faith, the vehicle that transports us along our spiritual journey and it is a gift from God. The rider balances and moves forward by seeking God, or "pedaling," for remaining stationary leads nowhere. The rider's understanding of who he or she is in Christ becomes clearer while pedaling forward toward the Cross.

The Christian's path is well marked, but at times it is dark and gloomy and difficult to see the surroundings. During these darker times the cross remains illuminated and easily spotted like when seen during the brightness of day. If I remain focused on the cross, my life will remain on the path. However, if I gaze too long into the forest lining the sides of the street my course will change and my bike will jump the curb resulting in me getting lost in a thicket where long thorns can tear and puncture the skin. Too far into the trees and my vision becomes obscured and ability to return to the path becomes compromised.

*Along the path and between the curbs are potholes (trials) that can cause a bouncy ride and maybe even cause the rider and his bike to wreck and fall, but the bike is **never too broken** to be picked up and pedaled again. The bike remains on the path during these temporary collisions; all that is needed to move forward again is the **will to get back on the bike and pedal**. Hitting potholes, falling off the bike, and getting back up strengthens a rider's character.*

*Initially, the rider bounces through many potholes along his journey, but over time he begins to avoid them, one by one. Avoiding every pothole throughout the ride is impossible, but steering clear of them becomes easier as the cross illuminates the path ahead with increasing brightness. Evading potholes with each turn of the handlebars creates change in the bike's direction. These **redirections** reveal views, or angles, of the path never observed before, which lead the rider to use the entire width of the path for traveling. He is surprised his sight of the cross is never lost nor his **forward** movement ever compromised after each turn. With every push of the pedal and pothole dodged his assurance in his cycling grows. At times he finds* *himself riding adjacent to the curb with its close view of the mysterious dense forest. To avoid jumping the curb he relies on two things: the hands grasping the handlebars and his focus.*

To whom do the hands belong? When I ask this question, I am usually met with a pause and then given varied responses. I'd like to think they belong to God. Each of us who has accepted the gift of a bike travel through life on it. Our paths take many different directions, depending on how tightly we hold onto the handlebars and where we fix our gaze. I would like to think at some point in our lives we trust God enough to give Him the handlebars. I am attempting to give my bike's handlebars back to God, realizing He is the only one who can guide me safely down the path and around the many potholes of impatience, pride, lack of kindness, boastfulness, and envy to name a few. My gaze remains focused on the cross.

Where is my path now heading? Have I previously jumped the curb? How do I find my way back? I am seeking to give up steering and allow God to guide my direction as I listen to Him through my prayers, Bible study, and changing heart. My potholes in the past seemed immense and were difficult to avoid. At times they were all I could see. I don't desire to fall to the ground and wreck again, Lord. Please guide me for I don't want to worry or be afraid, anymore.

Chapter 26

A Bag of Bones

September 20, 2010

> *"Father, into your hands I commit my spirit" (Luke 23:44).*

When the spirit leaves my bag of bones (my body) I'll die this age's death. Do I embrace my spiritual being today? Who wins the battle today of how I live my life? Will I allow the Spirit to live through me? My spirit is in me, and it's who I am. I don't want to fight anymore. Not I, but the Spirit who lives in me. May my spirit always be thankful, humble, and honorable to God. Hallelujah.

September 22, 2010

We die because of our sins. Christ died, yet He never sinned. Only one person has ever existed on this earth and had all the credentials to never die, for He had committed not a single sin in his life. Jesus. But He did die; far worse, He was put to death for crimes He never committed. Put to death by every human to ever inhabit the earth. Truly His death has to mean something. It does. It covered all the sins of those who believe in Him.

The lamb is the most innocent of animals. But Christ is more innocent. It is unfathomable to consider seeing a man's face on this earth and think he could be sinless. The Old Testament taught us man was incapable of remaining sinless, yet this man was capable of pulling it off. Certainly something amazing must have happened. I must get past an earthly vision of Christ, for He is of heaven, the incarnate and the transfigured.

Chapter 27

Today, I Am Here for You

Every creature in heaven and on earth ... singing to Him who sits on the throne and to the lamb be praise, honor, glory, and power forever and ever. (Revelation 5:13)

Each person was judged according to what he had done. (Revelation 20:13)

And God will wipe every tear from their eyes. (Revelation 7:17)

*My fear last May was related to dying, but more specifically, it was the process of how I was going to die and ultimately **where I would go** when it finally happened that petrified me. Assurance in my faith and His presence in my life are becoming tantamount in my thinking these days. I will keep searching, as the Potter's wheel is spinning ever faster.*

September 23, 2010

The following are responses of people when in God's presence and seeing His glory:

Were not our hearts burning within us while He talked with us on the road and opened the scriptures to us? (Luke 24:32)

And they stayed continually at the temple, praising God. (Luke 24:53)

And when God allows insight:

Then their eyes were opened. (Luke 24:31)

Then he opened their minds so they could understand the scriptures. (Luke 24:45)

I can be diligent in my studies, but until God wishes to reveal Himself to me, I won't understand. I pray He desires to reveal Himself. Lord, give me the eyes and ears to respond to You. Amen

*From where does love come? "Love, which comes from a **pure heart** and a **good conscience** and a **sincere faith**" (1 Timothy 1:5, emphases added).*

September 25, 2010

I have many thoughts in my head today about what I could do. I prayed and asked for direction. I then had a significant episode of palpitations, causing me to lie down, secondary to severe lightheadedness. Once again, I have no control over my life. I pray I continue to be patient as I observe what He reveals to me. May God, Christ, and the Holy Spirit have all the praise, honor, glory, and power for anything I do, say, or think in Their name.

While lightheaded and aware my ICD may go off again, I asked myself, "Do I desire to remain on this earth?" I do, but for what purpose? Do I love this world for what I get to do and what it provides me, or do I see what God wants me to do in it before He separates my spirit from this body?

I pray He will give me clarity to do what He wants me to do for Him. I hope I am reading things correctly, but I would like to spend the rest of my time on Earth accepting His purpose for me and following through by my actions according to that purpose. I know I do not know (never will) when my time on this earth (this age) ends, but today I am here and will seek Him diligently. May only His will be done!

"I spread out my hands to you; my soul thirsts for you like a parched land" (Psalm 143:6).

Chapter 28

Freedom

September 27, 2010

"Then you will know the truth, and the truth shall set you free"
(John 8:32).

Do I have anything to hide? Not any more. All is known.
*From the musical adaptation of the Victor Hugo novel, **Les Mis-**
***érables**, Jean Valjean, after witnessing another man being wrongly*
accused of a crime for which he himself was guilty, boldly proclaimed
his true identity to the police inspector, Javert. Valjean had spent
years avoiding authorities after being convicted of stealing food. He
tried justifying to himself why he should not confess and let the other
man be arrested. After all, he was now an owner of a factory with
many workers whose livelihoods would be threatened if he should go
to jail. His conviction and desire to do what was right pierced the bar-
riers to truth as he announced for all to hear, "I am prisoner 24601."
Afterward, the story illustrates Jean Valjean's redemptive process in
addition to his observance of the grace he received from God, which
released his enslaved heart.

"Set me free from my prison that I may praise your name"
(Psalm 142:7).

My strength is in You, Father. Thank You for that freedom. Please help me cast off the chains I place on myself today—the chains that limit the good acts You have already prepared for me.

"So that by His death he might destroy him who holds the power of death—that is, the devil—and free those who all their lives were held in slavery by their fear of death" (Hebrews 2:14–15).

Do I fear death any more? I feared death so much in May of this year after my first V tach episode. I feared leaving loved ones. I feared my faith wasn't adequate, as illustrated by the life I had lived. I feared not being accepted into the kingdom, and I feared eternal damnation. Only my faith in Jesus frees me from that slavery to fear death.

"Keeping our eyes on Jesus. The source and perfecter of our faith." (Hebrews 12:2)

"Have faith in God," Jesus answered (Mark 11:22)

It is not enough to just have faith, I must have faith in something— something that unlocks the gates, removes the shackles, conquers the walls, and splits the seas. Only one man in history has demonstrated this power and capability.

*I have faith in Jesus Christ, the real "something." Because of my faith in Christ **alone**, I know my heart is **forever** set free.*

When anyone is imprisoned or enslaved, he is consumed with having to please the warden, guard, or master to get (earn) access to every dimension of life, even survival. When he is finally freed, he enters a world filled with temptations. Without some type of protection or assurance, the newly freed person can easily be led back to prison because of temptation's false assurances and provisions. I think of the newly freed Jews from Egypt who had just witnessed the miraculous crossing of the Red Sea with Moses. As their patience grew thin, many complained that they had it better as slaves in Egypt and wondered if they should go back. Prison can create a distorted view of the world. An individual within its walls doesn't have to worry about where to eat, for that will be provided, or where to sleep, for that too will be provided. The amenities are provided, but at what cost? How much is forfeited for this false security?

Life is so much more than just surviving. I have to ask myself for what am I surviving? For what am I living? Is it to get to the next day, the next meal, or my next breath? Life is more than that. I desire more and God desires more for me too.

I am incrementally experiencing this renewed freedom. My bondage to the fear of death, how I am to die, worry related to the actions in my life and whether a person of faith can live such a life, and thoughts of past sins being too much to overcome are drifting away. I want them all to be gone—the blame, the guilt, and the fear. Walls are tumbling down, fences are being cut through, and waters are parting, all because of Christ's death on a cross atop a lonely hill called Golgotha.

I'm still on this earth, but I don't have to fight the same battles. How do I serve and please the One who is setting me free? It's a natural desire to show appreciation and thanks to Him who is freeing me, and I know none of my actions are required for my release. I want to show that I don't take His sacrifice for granted. I will be eternally grateful. Thank You, God. Amen.

As trials and resistance come my way from this world, I pray I will never lose sight of this freedom. If I remember the thoughtful face of the One who freed me, I know I will never have difficulty reclaiming my freedom. I don't know any other way now.

Chapter 29

One Big Pothole

Remember that illustration about the bike and the path with its potholes? Well, I hit a really big one on September 28, 2010.

September 29, 2010

> *Yesterday while sitting with Cindy in the kitchen, I had a significant heart irregularity, resulting in my turning pale and diaphoretic (sweaty). I also developed a distant look in my eyes, a look Cindy has grown to know all too well, but she said this one was really bad. She shows such strength during these times. I had great difficulty looking into her eyes yesterday, for when I did, it felt like I was saying good-bye.*

> *I have been having increasing symptoms the past few days, apparently due to multiple runs of V tach. All my heart's rhythm data is easily downloaded from my ICD. In a few days, I am supposed to go to Cleveland. I have to get there, for the Cleveland Clinic has a cardiac PET scan that will be critical for making my diagnosis and guiding therapy. Surely God wouldn't bring me this close and then not let me go!*

I was starting to think and act like Naaman, expecting only what *I* thought should be the appropriate course of action for managing my illness. But then ...

Now it is time to apply what I am learning. I will trust God to lead me. If the trip is canceled secondary to my condition, so be it. He will guide me in another way I haven't considered. Thank you, Father, for the peace that Your wisdom and love provides.

*I received a visit in my hospital room today from Donna (admitting director of the hospital) who had a CABG (coronary artery bypass graft) and received an ICD in the last year. She was shocked **eight times** due to a broken lead (wire) a few months ago. She now feels like she suffers PTSD (posttraumatic stress disorder). She probably does. She is recovering, but I could see the toll this has had on her. She lives each day to its fullest now, a common, repetitive theme with people who have had their ICD go off—especially multiple times!*

> *But let all who take refuge in you be glad; Let them ever sing for joy. Spread your protection over them that those who love your name may rejoice in you. For surely, O LORD, you bless the righteous; you surround them with your favor as with a shield. (Psalm 5:11–12)*

September 30, 2010

*Cindy shared Psalm 77 with me for encouragement. I particularly enjoyed verse 19. "Your path led through the sea, Your way through the mighty waters, **though your footprints were not seen**. You led your people like a flock by the hand of Moses and Aaron" (emphasis added).*

Today I met a housekeeper, Mary, at the hospital, who shared some of her life stories. She was born in a cemetery. I laughed so hard. I never know from whom the next story or insight will come. I have treasured my conversations with all the folks who told their stories when I needed to hear them most. Thanks Clarence, Jeffrey, Donna, Peggy, Grady, Jon, Mary, and Ann.

October 1, 2010

Do I desire to please God and seek His praise? Do I look for opportunities to show His goodness, much like a child tries to please his parents? Am I too proud to do the good things He has set out for me today? I will think about love today. What do I do that reflects love in the following ways (based upon 1 Corinthians 13:4)?

> *Is patient and kind*
> *Does not boast or envy*
> *Is not proud, rude, self-seeking, or quick to anger*
> *Keeps no record of wrongs*
> *Does not delight in evil*
> *Rejoices in the truth*
> *Always trusts, protects, hopes, and perseveres.*

"The goal of this command is love, which comes from a pure heart and a good conscience and a sincere spirit." (1 Timothy 1:5).

God is love!

October 3, 2010

Help me to fear You only, Lord, who can destroy the spirit, and not those who can only destroy things made from the dust of the earth. My spirit is from God and made from nothing. My body is made from dust.

My physical heart had reached a nadir, and my hope for a diagnosis was waning, but God had been preparing me for such a time as this. Since having V tach at my office in May, my dependence on God and my implanted electronic gear was clearly evident. I had never known a greater need for healing, physically or spiritually, than at this time. He had prepared my "hearts" to be probed, evaluated, and diagnosed. I was broken and needed to be fixed.

I was exactly where I needed to be.

II. Cardioversion

Chapter 30

Intensive Care

October 6, 2010

*Cindy and I are going to Cleveland today. Fortunately, I was well enough to be discharged from the hospital in San Antonio yesterday. I expect anything on this trip. I have prayed and know I am prepared for whatever happens. I can feel His presence. I read 1 Thessalonians today, where Paul leaves Thessalonica with this admonition: "**Always** be joyful, be prayerful **continually**, and give thanks in **all circumstances**" (emphases added).*

I am thankful for what I am getting to do today!

October 7, 2010

Today is the day I start my Cleveland Clinic experience. How joyful it was yesterday to go from San Antonio to Cleveland with no major problems. I had some irregularities in my heart rate, but thankfully they weren't severely symptomatic or compromising. I am amazed at what I now tolerate. My condition has deteriorated to the point that I had to be transported through the airports by wheelchair. I appreciated how kind the airline personnel were while transporting me from gate to gate.

It was weird being in the wheelchair. I didn't feel like I was in an airport. No decisions to make. I just moved from place to place unhindered and to the front of the line. No encumbrances, roadblocks, or obstacles obstructed my path. I just had to be quiet and let others do the thinking and pushing.

I wonder how many obstacles I have placed in the path God would have me go that have kept me from moving freely and unobstructed? How many roadblocks have interrupted my forward progress? In the past, I had intermittently sought God's guidance, but usually I went alone, under my own strength and with my own limited capabilities. How do I jump aboard the "Jesus wheelchair" and enjoy the ride He wishes me to take? As I go through my day today, I plan to incorporate Christ in all decisions. Amen.

I met my Cleveland Clinic electrophysiologist today, who is the chairman of the department of electrophysiology. That's right, the head of the department. The very one who I had discussed my case a couple of months ago found time to take care of me. **Thank You, God.** *Before I visited with him, I had to first see the pacemaker tech that evaluated and downloaded all my data from the ICD/pacemaker.*

The tech was quite bright and enjoyable. During the evaluation, she asked me what I was doing yesterday afternoon. I told her I was traveling through three different airports. She pulled her head back and said, "We don't see many like you around here." Now that was the last thing I wanted to hear from a place that treats rare cases from all over the world. She informed me that my heart had gone into V tach **thirteen** *times yesterday.* **Wow! I thank God for getting me to this place.** *I'm sure the folks who were sitting next to me on the two planes yesterday are thanking Him too.*

A view of Cleveland from the roof of the Cleveland Clinic.

"For as high as the heavens are above the earth, so great is His love for those who fear Him; As far as the east is from the west, so far has he removed our transgressions from us" (Psalm 103:11–12).

October 8, 2010

I'm getting ablation number three at eleven a.m. today (Friday). I found out yesterday from my cardiac PET scan that I probably have what my doctors back in San Antonio were thinking: sarcoidosis. The PET scan "lit up," or suggested, inflammation in my chest lymph nodes, heart, and upper lobe of my right lung. I discussed the results with a sarcoidosis pulmonary specialist who explained what my workup would entail, but first they wanted to get my heart calmed down with the ablation. Next Monday (in three days), his pulmonary colleague will perform a bronchoscopic (look down my windpipe) ultrasound-guided transtracheal biopsy of my chest lymph nodes. Boy, that was a mouthful. Sorry for the pun. A tissue diagnosis is needed to confirm sarcoidosis, so Cindy and I will have to stay a few extra days in Cleveland, but who cares after waiting months for a diagnosis. Once a diagnosis is made, I will finally start therapy, which will hopefully reverse this downward spiral of the past six months.

The following is a brief discussion of sarcoidosis from the National Heart and Lung and Blood Institute (www.nhlbi.nih.gov/health/health-topics/topics/sarc/).

Sarcoidosis (sar-koy-DO-sis) is a disease of unknown cause and leads to inflammation. This disease affects your body's organs. Normally, your immune system defends your body against foreign or harmful substances. For example, it sends special cells to protect organs that are in danger.

These cells release chemicals that recruit other cells to isolate and destroy the harmful substance. Inflammation occurs during this process. Once the harmful substance is gone, the cells and the inflammation go away.

In people who have sarcoidosis, the inflammation doesn't go away. Instead, some of the immune system cells cluster to form lumps called granulomas in various organs in your body.

Overview
Sarcoidosis can affect any organ in the body. How-
ever, it's more likely to affect some organs than oth-
ers. The disease usually starts in the lungs, skin and/
or lymph nodes (especially the lymph nodes in your
chest).

Also, the disease often affects the eyes and liver. Although
less common, sarcoidosis can affect the heart and brain,
leading to serious complications.

If many granulomas form in an organ, they can
affect how the organ works. This can cause signs
and symptoms. Signs and symptoms vary depend-
ing on which organs are affected. Many people
who have sarcoidosis have no signs or symptoms
or mild ones.

The outlook for sarcoidosis varies. Many people re-
cover from the disease with few or no long-term
problems. More than half of the people with sarcoi-
dosis have remission within three years of diagnosis.
"Remission" means the disease isn't active, but it can
return. Relapse (return of the disease) one or more
years after remission occurs in less than five percent
of patients.

Sarcoidosis leads to organ damage in about one-
third of people diagnosed with the disease. Damage
may occur over many years and involve more than
one organ. Rarely, sarcoidosis can be fatal. Death
usually is the result of problems with the lungs,
heart, or brain.

Poor outcomes are likely in people who have ad-
vanced disease and show little improvement from
treatment.

In a nutshell, there you have it. I don't like the part about which affected organs can lead to death. Hopefully, I will be one of those patients who go into remission quickly with treatment.

Since seeing my Cleveland Clinic electrophysiologist the other day, I have reduced my dosage of the drug Sotolol. He wanted my heart to be more sensitive, which allows for increased cardiac excitability during the ablation therapy. This possibly could help him locate the one or many sources of electrical ectopy. Being placed into a situation of increased vulnerability, allowing for a greater chance of having V tach, is quite unnerving.

God similarly wants me to "reduce the dosage" of my earthly idols for my consumption of them creates a false sense of security. Eliminating them makes me feel quite vulnerable, but unless I do, I won't experience the "excitable" state my spiritual heart needs in order for God to perform an "ablation" of the areas that are causing my separation from Him.

> *And this is the will of Him who sent me, that I shall lose none of all that he has given me, but raise them up at the last day. For my Father's will is that everyone who looks to the Son and believes in him shall have eternal life and I will raise him up at the last day. (John 6:39–40)*

How do I consume Christ daily? God is the Word, and the Word is in me. I accept the Holy Spirit. I believe Jesus is the human sacrifice promised by the prophets to save the world and bring salvation. I will be patient and wait on Him to return in His final glorious act to reign with goodness, justice, and power on this earth. I hope my daily actions are guided by His Spirit and by the mercy and grace I receive in a life filled with iniquity.

October 9, 2010

2:00 a.m.

AAAhhh! I took this picture with my phone.

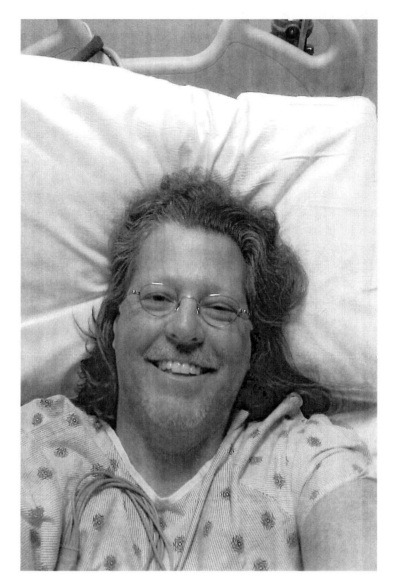

After Ablation in Cleveland Clinic at 2 am.

My cardiac monitor shows a calm chest with no noticeable irregular beats. The burning soreness after the five-hour ablation procedure yesterday is now gone. My chest (heart) feels like it got a complete tune-up. The two femoral (inguinal) blood vessel sites (one artery and one vein) look good with no hematomas or swelling.

My experience at the Cleveland Clinic has been outstanding. I understand why U.S. News & World Report has ranked them number one for cardiovascular services in the United States seventeen years in a row. I am thankful to God for the opportunity to be here.

6:30 a.m.

I sit on the edge of my hospital bed peering into the dark night just before sunrise anticipating I will get to live a different life today. I slept well last night. I know I still have the bronchoscopy in two days to determine if my lymph nodes have sarcoid, but I feel like I have a takeoff point at last to confront this illness. This has been a precarious existence the last five months, always feeling I could go into V tach at any time and not knowing if an irregular beat in my chest will lead to a more sustained V tach. Never swimming alone, always driving on the right side of the road in case I need to pull over suddenly, and feeling my ICD anti-tachycardia pace (ATP) me out of V tach episodes while hoping it will not shock me again.

My thoughts related to my illness have overwhelmed me at times. When will I ever start thinking about a healthy me again? What will I be able to do in the future? There are still too many questions about my illness and how, or if, I will respond to the upcoming treatments. At least today I feel I have a new start. I'm feeling better and am going to enjoy this day.

*This illness has shaken my faith to its core. But I wouldn't trade its intensity, which I haven't dealt with before, for anything, for I have been stagnating and dying spiritually for years. I have been performing perfunctory Christian duties, but not living the life. Never understanding that reading the Word and trying to do what it says **on my own** is impossible. I'm finally realizing I can't do what it says by just trying. Only by acknowledging God and asking Him to provide me with what I need will my faith truly be revealed for His purpose only.*

*I have developed a greater appreciation for what my true heart desires and yearns for more than anything else. **Desire** by John Elderidge discusses this idea clearly, and his story has blessed me greatly. I am also beginning to better understand what love means and how I can express it in my life toward God, others, and myself.*

I have committed Scripture to memory since May 5 and find it sooth-ing and enjoyable to recite. Three verses in particular have come to mean a great deal to me: Deuteronomy 20:3; Psalm 139:23–24; and 1 Corinthians 13:4–7. I try to recite these verses before getting out of bed each morning, as I want my heart to be set upon God before I do anything else each day. I am prone to talk to others about Christ these days, I've noticed. I share what He is doing in my life and am curious to hear what He is doing in theirs.

I have become increasingly concerned about whom I am helping and how I should spend my time, my life, and my money. I'm trying to learn to give from the impoverished areas of my life.

I remain hopeful for a cure, and if it comes, my desire is that it's pres-ence in my life and body will honor and glorify God. But if a cure doesn't come, I want my response to similarly honor Him as well. My hope is not in my earthly life, but in my spirit and the opportunity for my name to be written in the Book of Life.

God can still do many things through me whatever my physical ca-pacity. I will look to Christ and praise and honor Him. I look forward to the day He reveals His reign. I also pray for the saints who will die for the sake of Christ.

Chapter 31

A "Ten"

Oct 10, 2010, or 10/10/10

What a magnificent day, witnessing God's presence in my life. Yesterday evening after being discharged from the hospital, I felt as if I had the flu, but I had no fever. I felt better this morning after sleeping on and off last night. Cindy and I ate a late breakfast and then decided we would attend a service at a church down the street from our hotel, the Euclid Avenue Church of God.

Euclid Avenue Church of God.

The church had an eleven o'clock service, so we went. The congregation was predominantly black. All the women were sharply dressed, wearing hats and their best suits. Cindy and I sat in the middle and looked around at the pleasant faces and said hello. There were around 150 people total.

A very elegant woman named Betty Williams entered our pew and sat next to Cindy. She was eighty-nine years old and sharp as a tack. She greeted us and welcomed us to her church. (How she knew we were visiting I will never know.) She and Cindy discovered they shared the same last name (Cindy's maiden name was Williams), so they hit it off and were talking a mile a minute. After learning that we were in Cleveland for evaluation and treatment of my medical problem, Betty said they often had visitors from the Cleveland Clinic. Cindy also told her that I probably had sarcoidosis. I am always amazed how quickly two women can update each other about their entire lives.

Upon hearing my diagnosis, Ms. Williams suddenly stopped their conversation. She leaned forward, looked directly into my eyes, and said, "I have sarcoidosis too." She then pointed to four other congregation members who also had sarcoidosis, and one of them was the lead pastor! A chill ran down my spine as I considered the probability of sitting next to someone with sarcoidosis this particular day on this particular pew, surrounded by others with the same illness, including the lead pastor who would soon be preaching.

*I knew sarcoidosis was more predominant in blacks in the United States, but this chance meeting with Ms. Williams seemed very remote. Betty smiled and said, "You're the first **white** person I've ever met with sarcoidosis." I responded, "It is good to be with people of my **own kind.**" She laughed with her entire face. The service was starting, so we ended our conversation. **What else does God have planned for me today?** I sat back and with great anticipation waited on what was to come.*

The congregation sang and rocked like only a predominantly black congregation can, and I enjoyed it immensely. Many of the men spoke loudly during the service from their pews and encouraged the preacher with "Hallelujah," "Amen," "Okay," or "Watch out now, preacher." It was really fun, and I was tempted to say something, but I let my stiff "white side" come out and just listened. I thought of King David in 2 Samuel 6:14 when he was transporting the ark of God to the City of David wearing only a linen ephod (Hebrew priest's apron) dancing "before the Lord with all his might." I look forward to the day when I can worship so fully, but it wasn't going to be at the Euclid Avenue Church of God today. My loss.

During the two-hour service, I listened to the most impassioned prayer I have ever heard ad-libbed and later a fifteen-minute rendition of "Amazing Grace," which the soloist belted out in her amazing voice while bringing the congregation into and out of singing. It was so beautiful. I doubt that John Newton, who penned the words of this song and had been converted to Christianity as a sailor aboard a slave ship, ever imagined that someday a black woman in America would sing the words with such eloquence and grace. I know Mr. Newton is in heaven grinning from ear to ear.

The lead pastor, who I had just learned also had sarcoidosis, greeted the congregation and asked visitors to stand and introduce themselves. Cindy and I stood and announced our names and where we were from. We were greeted sincerely. Next, the minister acknowledged the church's reverence for God's Word and His presence in the building today. He stated, "He isn't always here, ya know, but He is today." I already knew.

The pastor said that he had a change in plans for the topic of his sermon. The previous week, he had told the congregation he was going to speak on the love between a husband and a wife in a Christian home, but instead, he felt led to speak on a topic that is a precursor to that love. He announced the new title for the sermon, "The Condition of Our Hearts." My jaw dropped. It felt like the breath had been knocked out of me, probably similar to what my son had experienced after getting nailed by that line drive last summer.

I felt God speaking directly to me at that moment, and it continued throughout the masterfully crafted sermon. The pastor shared so many Scripture verses related to the heart. He compared the physical and spiritual hearts and how each can become diseased. He then explained how they could be kept in shape: the physical heart through exercise, eating right, reducing stress, and getting regular medical checkups; the spiritual heart through practicing the spiritual disciplines of prayer, reading God's Word, fellowship with other

Christians, and service. Basic stuff, but boy, was it what I needed to hear. The pastor preached for I don't know how long, but I could have sat and listened all day. When I'm bored, I often look at my watch. But I didn't even look once.

The pastor started his closing remarks. He had quoted over twenty verses related to the heart throughout his sermon, but he chose one that would grasp and illustrate what he wanted us to hear. He cleared his voice and uttered the sweetest words I have ever heard from any pulpit,

> *Search me oh God and know my heart;*
> *Test me and know my anxious ways.*
> *See if there is anything offensive in me;*
> *And lead me in the way everlasting. (Psalm 139:23–24)*

*This is one of three verses I had memorized and recited every morning before getting out of bed since May 6, the day after my first episode of V tach five months ago. I began sobbing, for I **knew** God was with me and had not let go. This was the apical moment in regaining and understanding my assurance in Christ. **He hadn't let go!***

What are the odds of the pastor choosing this particular verse from the thirty-one thousand-plus verses in the Bible? I know the statistical probability contains many, many zeroes after the decimal point. PRAISE GOD!

God *did* speak that verse to me that day. I was in awe of all the "coincidences" during this challenging time: meeting Ms. Williams, the sermon and its ending verse, getting to Cleveland by wheelchair through three airports, thirteen episodes of V tach, and the *head* of the electrophysiology division of the cardiology department at the best cardiovascular center in the world *finding time* to take my case after previously telling me he couldn't. Each of these events punctuated what God did in my life that week. Topping it off, God provided me a diagnosis related to my physical heart and, more importantly, He revealed the problems affecting my *spiritual* heart. *And He did it all at the same time and in the same place.*

One of my goals the last five months has been to define my heart. This sermon helped me do that and see its condition. It also helped me to see what I need to do to get it into better shape. This type of event is rare in one's life, and when it happens, it remains on the brain forever. I am thankful for such a memory!

The sermon shared by Pastor Goode at Euclid Avenue Church of God and the events of the past five months leading up to this day have all been about my heart's condition, both spiritual and physical. The analogies between the two related to their workup, diagnosis, and treatment are remarkable.

First, my physical heart with its subtle, debilitating, enigmatic illness, compromising my ability to work, play, and even walk through airports. Its diagnosis required months of consulting with many dedicated physicians on unknown paths that challenged my progressively weakening state, but now a diagnosis is just moments away and soon treatment will begin that I optimistically anticipate will stop this disease's marching progression. I cannot predict my heart's responsiveness to treatment, but my hope is it will respond miraculously, and I will be able to give God all the glory for its cure.

*Next, my spiritual heart, which has been "defibrillated" from its near lifeless state and reminded that it, is **still alive**. Its diagnosis, requiring months of searching and being challenged while layers of hardening were removed, has now been revealed in the clarifying moments during the mornings, afternoons, and evenings spent alone praying to, searching for, and seeking God. The remedy was given in tolerable dosages to the patient and always with perfect timing.*

A major breakthrough occurred in therapy today resulting in a renewed assurance in my faith, salvation, and God's presence in my life—all things I have had since age seventeen but had sorely forgotten. Today, I boldly set forth on a renewed path with eyes resolutely fixed on the cross ahead!

The hymn Amazing Grace was eloquently sung today at church, It's second stanza, "T'was grace that taught my heart to fear, and grace my fears denied," illustrates the unmerited favor God has given me of which I am only beginning to comprehend.

I am writing of today's events while I sit in the warm sunshine this afternoon at a table near the Fahrenheit restaurant where Cindy and I will dine tonight in the Tremont area of Cleveland to celebrate this *wonderful day. I know today is not over and is filled with more possibilities. I will cast my eyes upon Him and seek His desire for me. Tomorrow I will deal with tomorrow. Thank you, Lord, for this **incredible day!***

Amen.

Chapter 32

THANKS!

October 11, 2010

> *I had my ultrasound-directed, transtracheal chest lymph node biopsy today. No complications. Thank You!*

October 12, 2010

> *I feel good today and am glad no study of my body is scheduled. No anxiety. I have prayed and read verses from the book of John. It's so easy to seek God in troubled times. I want to seek Him when I need Him most, and those are the days when I think I need Him **least**. May this be a day in which my thoughts, speech, and actions all honor Him, and may I return tomorrow with similar aspirations despite what I might do today to offend Him. His grace is immeasurable. Amen.*

October 13, 2010

> *For I am convinced that neither death nor life, neither angels nor demons, neither the present nor the future, nor any powers, neither height nor depth, not anything in all creation, will be able to separate us from the love of God that is in Christ Jesus our Lord. (Romans 8:38–39)*

Who shall separate us from the love of Christ? Shall trouble or hardship or persecution or famine or nakedness or danger or sword? (Romans 3:35)

Will I ever get to a point in which the promise of never being separated from God's love will give me the confidence and fearlessness to confront the challenges, battles, and controversies that lie ahead? I pray my faith will be adequate to respond to His leading. It is not I who will have the capability, but His Spirit in me.

October 14, 2010

Second day back home from Cleveland. I felt the pressure of the world coming down on me this morning around five. I finally thanked God for seeing me through the trials. I acknowledged I am incapable of masterfully handling anything or loving like I should unless He is doing the handling and loving. I prayed, acknowledged my sinfulness, and asked for His presence in my life today. A calmness settled over me as I went back to sleep.

Only by the saving grace of Christ and His willingness to hang on the cross am I able to receive God's forgiveness completely for all my waywardness. I am forever grateful to our King and Savior, Jesus Christ, the unblemished sin sacrifice on Calvary, and His triumphant conquering of death.

His story of salvation is the *only* way I know to reach heaven. I encourage anyone reading my story to seek God daily through the spiritual disciplines. Christ *must* be at the center of your worship, life, and faith.

That beautiful day in Cleveland (October 10, 2010, or 10/10/10), with its sunny skies and warm seventy-six degrees, I was blessed by the caress of God's love. I will always rank it a "10" on my memory scale. I stepped out of the church and knew God had directly spoken to me that day. He had a plan, but it looked a little different from what I had ever imagined. For years, I have struggled with decisions in my life because I was so weak in my heart regarding my relationship with Christ. Now as I move forward with a weakened physical heart caused by sarcoidosis, I step confidently ahead with a renewed and strengthened spiritual heart that has never known a greater love for God. What can ever separate me from that love now?

I consider it an honor and a privilege to be able to share this heart I have been given with each of you. I know it will always be sufficient for me and for those I meet daily. My prayer is that each of you will allow God to uncover your heart's condition and let Him have it totally every day for the rest of your life.

October 16, 2010

I am thankful for:

Righteousness through Christ's resurrection
My body being dead to sin
Having His Spirit living in me
Eternal life
Not having to fear the world
My life's journey and the presence of God in it
My family (Cindy, Morgen, Wil, parents, siblings, in-laws)
Friends
Opportunity to assist the formation of the Geneva School of Boerne
My education
Comfortable lifestyle and home
My health
My sufferings
Being a physician
Christ/Spirit winning over the sinful desires of my heart

And recently for:

Getting me through three airports while having V tach thirteen times
Expert medical care in Cleveland and San Antonio
ICD and pacemaker
Ablation therapy
Sunday morning (10/10/10) being a definite "10"
Transtracheal, ultrasound-directed chest lymph node biopsies
A diagnosis and treatment, and
                    Hope

Chapter 33

When It Rains It Pours

October 17, 2010

> *Is any one of you sick? He should call the elders of the church to pray over him and anoint him with oil in the name of the Lord"(James 5:14).*

I went to an elder (Mr. Weeks) at church and had him pray over me. He also had major heart disease and understood my plight. He said he would share my situation with the other elders.

Cindy, Morgen, and Wil were all baptized at the Guadalupe River with our church body (Oak Hills Church) around 3:30 this afternoon. It was a beautiful, sunny day in the mid-eighties. What a joy to witness and participate in the conversations related to their faith and decisions. Morgen and Wil each accepted Christ as their Lord and Savior a year ago. Cindy accepted Christ as a teenager while attending a Young Life camp called Windy Gap in North Carolina. She had been christened as a baby in the Catholic church but had never taken the "full plunge" of baptism. She wanted to be fully immersed, so why not with the kids? It was beautiful, and we all had a ball with the hundreds of others who were baptized that day.

Morgen, Wil, and Cindy getting baptized at the Guadalupe River.

Each day is filled with its many issues. I read a quote by Adrian Rogers from **What Every Christian Ought to Know Day by Day** *(B&H, 2007) today related to God's will for our lives. He states, "Jesus didn't come to get us out of trouble; He came to get into trouble with us. It doesn't mean we're out of the will of God when trouble comes. Don't get the idea that it's going to be all honey and no bees."*

Sometimes I think people feel when they are "right with God" no worldly devastation can fall upon them. This is a potentially dangerous way to think, as after working in the ER for years, I have seen devastation occur to many patients both Christian and non-Christian. And their friends and relatives were similarly devastated by the sudden loss of their family member or friend. Christians who think devastation shouldn't occur to them run the risk of feeling they have fallen from God's grace when misfortune occurs. But that couldn't be further from the truth. God uses misfortune everyday to build peoples' faiths ever stronger. It's all about where we look when misfortune occurs. God promises to provide a "way out" during these trying times. (1 Corinthians 10:14). Seeing the risen Christ helps us get through the trials.

October 19, 2010

> *What am I doing today to see God's love on Earth? My love for things of this earth will dissipate as I see His love more. Who is my neighbor today?*

October 20, 2010

> *Christ opened the eyes of a blind man. Please open the heart of a lowly sinner. I pray my eyes will radiate the light of Christ. Amen.*

October 23, 2010

> *I nearly passed out at a local restaurant while eating lunch with a good friend today. He knew I was bad off as he sat, paralyzed, watching me suffer through the event. I told him to call 911 if I should collapse.* **Just because my spiritual heart is mending doesn't guarantee the physical one is on the same path,** *I thought. I was hoping otherwise, though.*

> *Steroid (prednisone) therapy is currently the mainstay of treatment for my sarcoidosis. The problem is the sarcoid has affected an important organ (my heart) a lot, and its level of involvement may or may not respond to the current therapy. This is such a strange disease. Cardiac rhythms come and go as they please, causing symptoms from palpitations in the chest to severe lightheadedness or passing out, all while knowing each episode has the potential to cause death. I only have my defibrillator (ICD) to rely on if such an event occurs. Each time the rumbling in my chest erupts I wonder if the anti-tachycardiac pacing (ATP) function of my ICD will work or if I am going to be shocked (defibrillated) again. I feel sorry for those who watch me go through these episodes. I grow silent and glassy-eyed with a distant gaze (I am told) when they occur.*

> *The episode at the restaurant lasted a few minutes. Once I could stand up and walk, my friend drove me home. I sent my info from the ICD by phone to the EP cardiologist, who later informed me that I had had ten episodes of V tach over a forty-minute period, and in two of the episodes, my heart rate was 200–210 bpm. Hearing my rate is now going above 200 is concerning. I've noticed that my symptoms*

have become more ominous at a faster rate. It astonishes me that as an ER doc I can tolerate episodes of V tach and also discern the rate at which they occur. I never imagined anyone, much less me, would ever be able to say such a thing.

Later that afternoon, I met with the EP cardiologist, and we had a "heart-to-heart" discussion about his experiences with sarcoid-related heart patients. He stated that "some improved and some did poorly (died)." I asked about my scenario, and he indicated that my issues had grown "more significant."

The palliative effect of the ablation procedure to calm my heart at the Cleveland Clinic two weeks ago is wearing off and my San Antonio EP cardiologist doesn't expect to see much improvement from steroid therapy for four to six weeks. He said if I have another episode like I had today, I would need to be admitted. I don't want another episode like that ever again, nor do I want to be readmitted to the hospital. My current problem, however, is while waiting for the inflammation of the sarcoid to subside, I have to get my heart rhythm stabilized.

Dealing with my rekindled V tach this week has been stressful, and just when I thought I had all I could handle, I received news my parent's caretaker at their assisted living center in Boerne committed suicide by shooting herself in the head. She was found in front of the assisted care residence. I have had to frantically look for a new assisted living center for my demented father and aging mother who both use walkers. Cindy and I prayed for an answer and were guided to an assisted living center called New Hope, a wonderful place managed by a transplanted Romanian Christian family. We will transfer them both next Monday. Hallelujah. Finally, we are able to take a breath.

I am overwhelmed by the hardship thrust in my family's direction this last month. My illness, to and from Cleveland, the recurrence of V tach, learning my younger sister-in-law has developed seizures this week secondary to brain metastases originating from colon cancer, and now this awkward situation with my parents. Sin and its consequential misery cause havoc on this earth! So many are in need of Christ. My desire to share God's love and compassion has been a blessing throughout all these trials. The genuineness of the gospel has never been more real. I do cry some these days due to the palpable hurt and over-whelming suffering, but I stand steadfast, for nothing can separate me from the love of Christ.

Chapter 34

One More Time

I was admitted to the hospital today. I've been having multiple severe episodes of V tach since this morning. We were supposed to move my parents to the New Hope Assisted Living today. Cindy (incredible Cindy) had to drive me to the hospital through tears of frustration. I cannot express the admiration, love, and joy I have from witnessing her throughout her life trying to please God in all she does. I will do everything I can to let her know she is a joy in God's sight. I am honored to be her husband.

Observing Morgen watching me this morning was difficult. Her beauty is increasing daily, but her inner beauty is expanding far more. I see a heart opening up to God and wanting to yield to His teaching and direction. Her tears rip me apart when I feel the weakness and irregularity of my heart. She sees the distant look in my eyes and my pale appearance, feeling helpless and knowing I am completely dependent on my ICD's performance. I forget what she and Wil are going through with their dad. It has to be difficult.

Wil's sixteenth birthday is in two days. He is such a great kid. Smart and sensible with an ever-increasing heart for others and for God. I hope to encourage him, although my critical nature can get in the way sometimes. He is headed in the right direction. I look forward to witnessing the man he'll become.

I delight in thinking about my children's futures. It hurts too much thinking I might not be a part of them, especially given the direction I seem to be heading.

I was told I have had sustained V tach twenty-three times since last Tuesday. I knew I hadn't been feeling well, but with my mother and father's situation, I needed to get things done, so I plowed ahead. I've been told that it takes prednisone four to six weeks to start having an effect on reducing the inflammation of sarcoid. I'm not sure I have that much time since the rhythm problem is worsening.

When I was admitted to the hospital, the Medtronic technician came into my room and downloaded all the information from my ICD/PM. The concern on his and my EP cardiologist faces was disturbing, and I could tell things were getting much worse, especially when I observed the fireworks-type pattern of my heart's rhythm on the monitor. The aggressiveness of my therapy was about to be shifted into a higher gear. Time to throw off the gloves. It's time to rumble.

Tonight, they started me on an IV drug called amiodarone, for the frequency of serious V tach episodes was significant. I think everyone has hoped to not use this drug, for it has many potential side effects, ranging from severe pneumonitis (lung inflammation) and thyroid suppression to visual changes caused by crystals forming in the corneas, each of which are potentially irreversible. I will be transferred to another hospital today, I've been told, that has an increased capacity to handle any special needs I might have. I am also going to need consultation with the transplant cardiologist again.

I am beginning to see the possibility of needing a heart transplant someday. I reflect back on the sermon by Pastor Goode in Cleveland about "how God doesn't go in and mend or fix the spiritual heart, but rather He must go in and perform a complete spiritual heart transplant." My spiritual heart transplant occurred years ago at seventeen years of age, but I guess if He wants to continue with my physical heart, He can do as He pleases.

I pray my story about these events will honor Christ. My life has often been spent serving things with no merit. I hope each day I will seek to serve Him only. I pray for healing, but only healing that brings praise, honor, and glory to God! Amen.

Chapter 35

Assured

October 26, 2010

> *"Now my heart is troubled, and what shall I say? 'Father, save me from this hour?' No, it was for this very reason I came to this hour. Father, glorify your name!" (John 12:27).*

*What hour am I in **now**? How will my Father be glorified by this hour? My life has a purpose: to illustrate the love and person of Christ to whatever part of the world He wants to touch through me. Today I am nothing more than a servant needing to follow through with the day's tasks for my Master. If I know my Master, I will know what to do. I am thankful my good Master reveals Himself so completely. I pray for forgiveness related to my lack of desire and effort to know Him in the past and in the future. I hope the renewing of my mind will enable me to do what pleases Him.*

> *"Whoever serves Me must follow me; and where I am, my servant also must be. My Father will honor the one who serves me" (Romans 12:26).*

How do I serve Christ today? May I have the heart, soul, strength and mind to completely serve God. Who is my neighbor today?

I have been encouraged today and have had opportunities to encourage and share God's activity in my life.

"This is the day the LORD hath made. Let us rejoice and be glad in it" (Psalm 118:24).

Cindy is struggling. Feeling depleted and needs help. Lord, please show me what to do to help and encourage her today. She is your servant. Refresh her with Your Spirit. Please show me what to do.

October 26, 2010

No divided heart
No looking back
Truth only

October 27, 2010

Blessed assurance
Jesus is mine.
Oh what a foretaste
Of glory divine!
Heir of salvation,
Purchase of God,
Born of the Spirit,
Washed in His blood.

*(**Blessed Assurance,** First Verse, by Fanny Crosby and Phoebe Knapp, 1873)*

What insight and joy is revealed through this beautiful hymn. I will recite it throughout the day.

"Being confident of this very thing, that He who has begun a good work in me will complete it until the day of Jesus Christ" (Philippians 1:6, emphasis added).

Chapter 36

A "Window's View"

October 27, 2010

I wonder if I really grasp what I should do today? I know I am attempting. My service to God may primarily be in the hallways of hospitals for a while. I will patiently wait and see what He desires.

I met Irma today at the hospital while she was cleaning a room. Her mother died when she was nine years old, and her dad died even sooner. After her mother's death, she was raised by her older sisters, who, she said, "Didn't spend much time with me." She gladly accepted invitations to her neighbors' homes for dinner, but she always knew, even at a young age, that she was intruding and was not to wear out her welcome.

Irma believes in Christ. From her communication, I could tell she has scars from childhood. As an adult she has had her trials also. She divorced her high school sweetheart after thirteen years of marriage due to his worsening alcoholism. Having gone through all this, she still is able to proudly share that she has raised four beautiful children who have all done very well. The sparkle in her eyes expresses her love, pride, and full life.

I love the windows I get to peer through and the images revealed these days. Irma's story is such a window, which allows a brief but clear view into life and the world. My illness is also a pane I gaze through, allowing me to witness new images I've never seen. My response to the view is quite different now that it is based upon God's perspective and not just mine.

I used to say I loved the ER because it provided me a similar window to view the world, as if I would be wiser by observing, but for many years I didn't seek God's perspective when there. I became detached from the lives passing through it, and my surveillance and reactions were based solely on my perspective, not God's. Wisdom comes by seeking and fearing God in the midst of living life. So much of my past was not actively engaged with God during my long days and nights in the ER, and as a result, I missed significant lessons.
I'm so ashamed of my feeble life and lack of effort to please God. I have been so resistant to His open arms. He has placed my transgressions so far away, as far as the east is from the west. I don't understand why He loves me so much.

*While in the hospital, my thoughts abound, and although I want to stay positive and not be morbid, I have to start considering my death someday. I have always known that I'm going to die, but for some strange reason, I didn't think I would go through the death **process.** Anxiety triggered by the grotesque and terrifying manner death can present itself, as I have observed in emergency rooms, is always on the doorstep of my mind and wants to place its foot inside the door of my thinking. All I can do is proclaim, "Get back, Satan. In the name of Jesus Christ, leave this place!" Whatever pain, last gasping breath, or incoherent stare I must experience during this process, I will consider it a small price for what He has given me.*

*I will leave this earth someday. When will I leave? I don't know, perhaps sooner than I thought given my current condition. I know I have selfishly wanted to live to ninety or one hundred years of age while still having a full life, but "a full life" has taken on new meaning, and it doesn't seem to be measured in **years** any more.*

Life, whether full or not, is just that: life. No beginning, no end. There are variations on the theme and how we experience it, but I can no longer place it in a container with limits and bounds, as it is limitless and without boundaries. That's how God, who lives in me, wants me to live. I am thankful for His allowing me this time to seek Him and hopefully renew my mind and orientation. I am starting to see His grace and mercy. Amen.

Chapter 37

Spiritual Cardioversion

October 28, 2010

A thought I had today:

*Make sure what you **have** isn't interfering with what you need. Think about it, and if needed, get rid of some of the **haves.***

Great talk with Pauline today. She is a former workmate who witnessed my running many medical "code blues" at the hospital where we worked together years ago. She now works at the medical center where I am currently hospitalized. She shared her story about watching her husband die from Lou Gehrig's disease at the age of forty-one, leaving her with four children to raise. She is a devout Christian with a sincere heart. I appreciated her time and encouragement.

I just read Psalm 103 again. I love this psalm. I laughed at verses thirteen and fourteen: "As a father has compassion on his children, so the LORD has compassion on those who fear him; for He knows how we are formed, He remembers that we are dust" (emphasis added).

Oh, how I have tried to make myself much more than dust. Gaining more appreciation for the Spirit within the dust is making all the difference. I love that my God knows the simple nature of my being. I think of how a small child's behavior is so predictable by a parent. How often I must have thought I was too complicated for God to understand. What an arrogant fool I can be. I am but a child. Thank You, God.

I calculated the percentage of having my illness. Ten out of one hundred thousand caucasians get sarcoidosis. Five percent of those get clinical cardiac symptoms. (Vishal Sekhri et al. Cardiac sarcoidosis: a comprehensive review, Arch Med Sci. 2011 August, 7(4): 546–554)

$10/100,000 = 0.0001$

5% of $0.0001 = 0.05 \times 0.0001 = 0.000005$, or 5 per 1,000,000

There is nothing in this world I can hide from or avoid. Nothing. God, You have all of me. Amen.

October 29, 2010

A.M.

*I pray my life will reflect my understanding of the enormity of Christ's sacrifice on the cross. He saw the absolute evil in my past and future acts and still placed Himself as a sacrifice even though **He had the power** to avoid it all. How will I express my gratitude today? How will I be used for His kingdom? Is this the day He wants me in heaven or to minister to a lonely soul? His desire for me is my goal. His timing is more crucial than mine. He gets to do with me as He pleases, and I do not worry, for He is a good and merciful God. I am comforted by all the situations, encounters, and trials he allows me to experience along this path of righteousness He has guided me for His name's sake. Amen.*

P.M.

I am home after being discharged from the hospital tonight with the usual feebleness after lying around the hospital for five days hooked to monitors and IVs. I am now released to the "unmonitored" outdoors with no umbilical cord and hoping all will go well. Again, with any "freedom" upon release, there are vulnerabilities. I have occasional PVCs in my chest and wonder if I'm going into V tach. I was told to go back to the hospital if it does occur. Since Cindy was home with Wil, who was having his sixteenth birthday party, a good friend drove me home. Thanks, Peggy!

Anxiety penetrated my mind as I sat in the passenger seat during the ride home up Interstate 10. A wreck or even the threat of one could cause my catecholamines (adrenaline) to rev up and put me into V tach. After all, it only took a hot shower in the past. I thought about the doctor telling me to always have someone accompany me in the shallow or deep end of the pool in case I needed to be pulled out. Also, I think about my developing symptoms on a lone stretch of highway with no sophisticated medical center nearby that could handle my problem. My physical world is closing in.

October 30, 2010

Poor sleep last night after getting home, but it's great to be home and with the kids and Cindy. I napped for a couple of hours on the couch next to our open front door. Feeling the breeze and hearing the outside world moving about was so pleasant. In the hospital, the outside world stops, and you become consumed with thoughts related to your illness, nurse and doctor visits, IVs, meds, studies, procedures, and the constant distorted sound of the TV through the bedside speaker.

I'm on high doses (60mg/day) of the steroid prednisone, which can make a person feel crazy, and it disturbs my sleep pattern greatly.
I did something that was long overdue tonight. I knelt down next to my bed and prayed. My knees were hurting when I got up.

Oct 31

Picture from my journal illustrating the dream.

*During the wee hours of the morning, I had a special dream that seemed more like an image (as drawn in my journal above). It included a sapphire-bejeweled night sky lying atop rolling green hills. A blanket of gray clouds rested above, containing a single, small opening in which bright sprays of light radiated downward. In the distance, I could see a person with a glowing gold crown resting on his body reclining on his back on one of the hills. From the hill, the person and crown suddenly shot upward at a diagonal to the opening in the clouds. **Poof!** The dream was over.*

*I am grateful for the image. I feel it represents my assurance in being a member of God's kingdom and having my name written on a wall in heaven. After I awoke and considered the gift I have been given, I cried. I then prayed, thanking God. I broke down again, crying violently like I had never done before. While I was crying, I had a vision of Christ, and He was smiling at me. **I have never imagined Him being pleased with me.** What joy that smile gave me. The assurance of His love for me was overwhelming!*

*Later this morning, a thought entered my mind. I envisioned a piece of typing paper with a dot in the center made by the sharpest lead a pencil can have. It was almost impossible to see. The piece of paper represented my whole life—spiritual, emotional, psychological, and physical—and the dot represented the tiny place in my life I hold onto **just for me**. I share this place with no one else and try to hide it from God. This dot can no longer exist in my life! I can no longer hide from God, no matter how miniscule the place may be. I will be known, all truth will prevail, and it will set me free.*

Currently, I can't even hide from an illness that affects 5/1,000,000 persons. I freely give my "speck" to You, Lord, and thank You for allowing my "sheet of paper" to be white as snow. I confessed my sins as fully and totally as possible last night, and once again, I acknowledged Jesus Christ as my personal Lord and Savior. I acknowledged His sacrificial death on the cross and His glorious resurrection. He sits at the right hand of the Lord Almighty. Looking up now and seeing Christ with a smile is the most welcoming view of heaven I have ever known. I pray I never lose site of it again. Amen.

My life was not the same anymore. I had been given a clear view of my past with all its shortcomings, weaknesses, mistakes, blemishes, and sinfulness, yet I never felt freer from the bondage I was under for so long. A feeling I remember having as a young man after receiving Christ but somehow lost over the years. The consequential effect of my sinfulness and its associated behavior since accepting Christ has stunted my spiritual growth. Where was my physical heart with sarcoidosis headed at this time? I wasn't sure, but I knew my spiritual heart had received a new direction with a clearer path. All I had to do was trust and follow it.

I listened to a song by Bebo Norman named *Middle* from his album entitled *Ocean* numerous times this past year. Its message described the way I had felt for many years. Always feeling stuck *in the middle* between my human existence and spiritual being. Here is the first verse and refrain. (All Rights Reserved. Used By Permission)

It's as if You could find me anywhere
That I could go, to try to hide my thoughts from You
But just like some runaway I'm leaving here
With half a mind that hopes of getting caught

So we can just drive home in the dark
Where we'll let our, our feelings fly
They'll cut like shame to break me down again
Until there's nothing left but for me to tell You I'm, I'm sorry

But I don't wanna go home now
Stuck here in the middle alone now
Everybody's singing their song now
But I'm still reeling

I'm not trying to run away from
This beautiful life I've been given
I'm not looking for freedom
Maybe just a little meaning here in the middle

I didn't want to "go home" last May after my first V Tach episode, but much has changed since that fearful day. I don't feel "in the middle" anymore.

III. Recovery

Chapter 38

Recovery/Resuscitation

November 1, 2010

> *(I tell you the truth) those who listen to my message and believe in God who sent me have eternal life. They will **never** be condemned for their sins, but they have **already** passed from death into life. (John 5:24, emphases added)*

> *I am the LORD your God, who takes hold of your right hand and says to you, "Do not fear, I will help you." (Isaiah 41:13)*

November 2, 2010

Today, I had a wonderful chat with my friend John at Bear Moon. He is the friend with an ICD who I called from my car after I was defibrillated back in August. For some reason, we shared stories recounting our relationships with women in our youth and the associated awkward moments. I shared my story of my first sexual experience. He described it as a "tender story" and a tear came to his eye, which isn't easy for a seventy-three-year-old East Texan, ex-CEO of a major company, frog-giggin', 'coon-huntin' man who happens to be an old Ag (graduate of Texas A&M University). I was deeply touched by his sensitivity and comforted by our conversation.

I hadn't been to Bear Moon for some time, and that morning, I saw many of my old friends (some Christian, some not). We hugged. Many said they had been praying for or thinking about me. It was difficult to hold back tears. Again, I was very comforted.

I really need to rest every afternoon now or my heart will grow erratic. I fell asleep today, a classic, crisp, beautiful fall day with the smell of a changing season in the air.

*I was awakened by a dream. (Yeah, another one). I was with my eighty-five-year-old, moderately demented father at a pharmacy waiting at the counter when an elderly lady slumped over while sitting in a chair next to the pharmacist's counter. After a couple of short shallow breaths, she seized and then vomited. I went to her and laid her on the floor. She then vomited on me. I noted she no longer had a pulse, so I started CPR, thinking, **How is my heart going to take this**? I wanted to scream, "Does anyone know CPR?" but I couldn't get out more than a whisper. My father was asking, "What are you doing on the floor, son?" At that moment, I woke up. My heart was racing greater than one hundred bpm, but it slowly settled down as I collected myself. Wow, what a dream! I wonder if it meant anything?*

*I am familiar with managing resuscitations while simultaneously providing care for multiple patients in the ER. I often felt like the man on the Ed Sullivan show who could balance and spin plates atop multiple sticks at the same time. My dream reminded me that I am unable to do everything on my own now like I once did. I have learned that my capability to do the things I **need** to do is always possible through Christ who strengthens me. I just need to let go of the things I **want** to do, which don't coincide with God's will for me. My physical dependence on medications, ICD/pacemaker, and other people is increasing, and I'm now qualified for disability insurance. My growing dependence is not easy to accept and is forcing me to see through a different lens. I am forced to take twists and turns on my journey I wouldn't have necessarily taken before. Today, I have to see what Christ desires of me in whatever condition I find myself.*

My focus for so long has been saving physical bodies from the grips of death, but it is changing. My focus has now expanded to see-

ing lives saved for Christ. My ability to work in the clinics has been altered significantly, but my availability and capability to do what Christ would have me do has been richly expanded, and for that I'm extremely thankful.

I don't know what lies ahead, but I know I will continue to listen for and follow God's voice. Something has got to give in my life. My body is currently incapable of going to work in the clinics. I haven't worked now for three months.

The human body is not supposed to go into V tach hundreds of times and be defibrillated and anti-tachycardia paced (ATPed) a total of 110 times over six months with twenty-three of them successfully occurring in one week and still be writing about it. I'm not special, but by all accounts (according to my emergency medicine background), I should be dead. But I am alive in Christ and my spirit lives in this "bag of bones" called my body. I am living hour to hour now as I patiently seek His guidance.

After rereading these past few paragraphs and knowing steroids can cause mania (psychological term related to an individual having an elevated perception of self associated with what is called pressured speech and often overzealous religious overtones), I can see how someone might question where I'm headed. This very real potential side effect is not what is happening to me, and Cindy knows it too. We both monitor my behavior closely, for Cindy has witnessed this side effect with her father who was on a course of high-dose steroids before he died. I'm not sure what state I need to be in to learn what God desires of me, but I am thankful for the current state I find my-self and the next one and the one after that too.

> "Do not let your heart faint. Do not be afraid. Do not tremble or be terrified, for the LORD your God is He who goes **with you** to fight **for you** against your enemies, to **save you (or to give you victory)**" (Deuteronomy 20:3–4, emphases added).

Praise be to God and my King, Jesus. Amen.

Chapter 39

A Hospital Visit, Volleyball Game, Lecture, and Three Atheists

November 5, 2010

> *I'm spending a lot of time around the house these days and am encouraged by what God is revealing to me hourly: a particular Bible verse, a vision in a dream, various thoughts, even a phrase from a Bebo Norman song.*

> *I have enjoyed the people God allows me to spend time with these days too.*

November 6, 2010

> *I awoke this morning with a strong desire to visit a hospitalized friend who happens to be a chef. I have gotten to know him over the past couple of years via his restaurant and also in a very personal way: I've been his physician. He's a California dude and how he found Boerne, Texas, I am not sure, but given the way he can cook and manage a restaurant, I am glad he found it. It's a Saturday, and I had the day to myself, as Morgen and Cindy were at a horse show and Wil was doing something (like all sixteen-year-olds) all day. As per my usual routine, I recited my three verses in bed, spent some time in prayer, and read my*

Bible. Afterward, with the freedom I had this day and since I was feeling a little better, I committed my entire day to God whole-heart-edly.

*Off I went to the hospital. I had a great conversation with my friend and spoke briefly of my own experience this past year and how certain verses from the Bible were daily encouragement. He openly welcomed the discussion, and I was thankful. I will pray for other opportunities to speak with him. I gave him a book of verses related to different topics for men. I then felt it was time for me to go, so I said good-bye. That very moment, his mother and twin brother walked in. **Perfect,** I thought. **God's timing.***

*After leaving the hospital, I remembered the Geneva School of Boerne was playing in the state TAPPS 1A volleyball championship in San Antonio. I was feeling up for it, and the gym where they were playing happened to be fairly close to the hospital. They ended up winning, but unfortunately, it took them five games to do it; midway through the fourth game, I felt weary, and my heart was fluttering from the excitement. I **knew** I had to leave. I sat outside the arena a few minutes until I felt calm. A friend saw me leave; concerned, she checked on me. Those little moments are so refreshing. Thanks, Amy.*

During this period after my most recent hospitalization, I was starting to listen to my body, mind, and heart more than I ever had in my life. I was attempting to disallow the world and its neediness from taking me away from what I knew I *should* do. I was enjoying my day, committing each second to God, which was new for me. Comfort washed over me, much like when I was going through the airports by wheelchair the previous month, not worrying about gates, ticket lines, or crowds. I liked this sensation—a lot!

My friend Robert, who had witnessed my episode at the restaurant last month, texted me the final score of the volleyball game as I drove back to Boerne. Watching the parents and students, who have been growing with Geneva since its infancy, cheering on their championship team was awesome and inspiring. The school now has over five hundred students, grades K-12, which is a significant jump from our first year with thirteen (kindergarten, first grade, and third grade) students. I am extremely happy how God has blessed Geneva. Thank You, Lord!

*During the drive home, I remembered that a man was speaking to-day about his faith journey at the Boerne Grill at three p.m. I had read about the meeting in **The Boerne Star**. I went home, and after taking a short nap and feeling more rested, I went and listened to the new author.*

I asked him a few questions. He had been a devout atheist for more than fifty years. He was an intellectual and had worked as an electrical engineer his whole working life, but he never had a relationship with God. I believe that his profession of faith was genuine. I sat for an hour, listening. I then dismissed myself before he was finished speaking, for I knew it was time to leave. He gave me his book, and I gladly accepted it.

I stepped out to the street, preparing to go home, when I remembered my eighty-plus-year-old artist friend Bill, who still rides a Harley, was having an art show at his studio. It was one of those "Chamber of Commerce" sorts of days, so I thought, why not? Off to his studio I went, which was located in an old house.

There were numerous people inside, so I sat outside on the porch and waited for the crowd to thin out. I petted his cat LC (Lap Cat) and admired a gorgeous painting displayed on the front porch. That one painting was all I needed to see. I have a similar painting by Bill hanging in my dining room.

Bill has been a patient of mine, and I have enjoyed our evolving friendship over the years. He is a hard-edged, crusty old guy (he'd be the first to say so) with a good heart and a love of beauty that he shares with others through his paintings. He sat down with me, and I shared with him my medical issues, for he recognized I didn't look too great. I held back tears as I shared the trials of the last few months. He said, "Dying is supposed to happen to old farts like me, not you young ones." I could tell my presence saddened him, and I started to question why I had even gone to his studio.

Three of Bill's long-time friends had traveled to Boerne from far away: one from Utopia (no joke) and a husband and wife from Round Rock, north of Austin. They were having wine (not too much) and were enjoying the show on this crisp fall afternoon with their old friend. They were intellectual, fun loving, devout, dyed in the wool atheists. I told them, "I have no desire to debate any of you about evolution today," and we all laughed. As the patrons left the studio, we sat with Bill on the porch and shared bits and pieces of our lives, our appreciation of art, and our interests.

The man from Utopia had a love of "medical things." He is a nationally recognized artist who had studied at Yale and has a gallery in Houston. After he discovered I was a physician, he ran out to his car and brought back a faxed surgeon's report, describing in great detail his father's recent laminectomy (back surgery). He asked if I would explain the report's contents. I obliged and discussed what I felt comfortable with. He appreciated the information. He was intelligent, inquisitive, and an excellent listener—the kind that makes the speaker feel really important.

*He and his friends wanted to know about my background, and I told them I was a Christian. I spoke of my past briefly and then Bill chimed in about by most recent past. **Uh oh**, I thought. **I really don't want to get into that discussion with folks I just met.** They insisted I share my story, but I had to watch it, for the topic is so emotional for me. I said a quick prayer, asking God to help me turn off the waterworks while I told His story as it related to my life to a bunch of atheists.*

It was magical. I even got to the story about the Euclid Avenue Church of God and the assurance God gave me through Ms. Williams and the pastor. They listened intently. After sharing my story, I felt exhausted, so we hugged and shook hands, and they thanked me for sharing. I headed out to my car, knowing it was time to leave. When I opened the car door, the book the author at the Boerne Grill had just given me was on the front passenger seat—the story of a former atheist of fifty years and the path he took to find Christ. Immediately, I picked it up, went back to the studio, and explained to all of them that I had not read the book, but that it would be remiss for me to not share this incredibly timed acquisition. I was very excited, which they could see on my face. They gladly received it, and the woman said her husband would probably read it since he was a "searcher." So who knows?

I do know throughout today I sought God and looked for His presence in my life. I wanted Him to use me for His purpose. I can truly say my desire today was to listen, acknowledge Him in all things, be His instrument, and thank Him. I pray for each of the souls I met today. I got to let my spirit, through the Holy Spirit, interact with them, and it was great. I know I was nothing more than a brief moment in these people's lives, but I hope God will take that moment and amplify it to His glory. Thank You, Lord Jesus, for Your amazing grace and mercy. Amen.

Chapter 40

We All Have a Path

November 7, 2010

Jesus reached out to the sick, poor, downtrodden, weak, hungry, hopeless and gave them hope in salvation and eternal life. All that they will ever endure on this planet will not be all there is in their life. I can endure all pain and suffering with God's strength within me. Thank You, Lord. Amen.

*This year I continue to search for my heart and how I define it. John Elderidge, in his book **Desire,** describes the heart as "The deepest yearning I have inside of me, my deepest desires … It's the place where pain and joy share a common spot."*

What do I seek when Christ asks me, "What do you want?" like he asked the paraplegic at Bethesda, the two blind men along the side of the road, and the Samaritan woman at the well. I am starting to get a clearer picture of my answer, and best of all, it originates deep within my heart.

I want to live fully in Christ's love while living on this earth. I want to shed the useless desires of my life that interfere with my sincerest desires, which are most critical for experiencing Christ's love for me. I want to experience joy and that be the reason I choose my actions, not out of fear of consequences. I want the joy David expressed. I don't want to be limited by what the world knows to be "correct." The Pharisees knew the Bible (Old Testament) better than anyone, but where was the joy in their moralistic lives that was governed by the law? Why would most of them not respond to the teachings of Christ? I want to be vulnerable to Christ's teachings.

My desires, which guide my actions, should consider the joy associated with the act. My desires may be too many, so I will ask God to whittle them down to what He wants for me. From now on, my heart will only seek joy through Christ and not through a world filled with dutiful obligations that may or may not make me happy.

> Ask and it will be given to you, seek and you will find, knock and the door will be opened to you. (Matthew 7:7)

> I have come that they may have life and have it to the fullest. (John 10:10)

> Be joyful in hope, patient in affliction, faithful in prayer. Share with God's people who are in need. Practice hospitality. (Romans 12:12–13)

> Rather, clothe yourselves with Lord Jesus Christ, and do not think about how to gratify the desires of the sinful nature. (Romans 13:14)

November 11, 2010

Help me, Lord, assist others as they travel along their paths. I am tired of being so insecure that I feel the need to direct another's path. Who am I to have any idea as to the various paths You have prepared for each individual? I pray I never hinder or stand in the way of that path. Please help me to remain silent and speak only when You desire. Sometimes only supportive prayer, performing an act, or just listening is required of me. Help me to be patient for Your timing in others' lives.

I was so refreshed by Zachariah (his prophesies related to Christ) and by James, Chapter 1 today. Please, Lord, help me to believe in all I ask for and remove double-mindedness from me. You brought people back to life, healed the very sick, and enabled paraplegics to stand and the blind to see. Why have I limited You so? Forgive me for my lack of faith. I give it all to You, Lord. You are worthy of all praise. Take my sarcoid away, Father. Take away the need for wires and the defibrillator. Heal this heart. All miracles I have read in the Bible point to Christ. My healing can only do the same.

No bargaining, Lord. Your will be done. I will persevere through this trial and look forward to my hope in Christ. I pray You give me continued opportunities to share the love You have shared with me. I am daily (hourly) touched by the most sincere blessings You have bestowed on me. As I look back on my past, You have always been there to redirect. I thank You for this opportunity to have a greater appreciation for and insight into my faith. And thank You for giving me the faith I have. In Christ. Amen.

What a week it has been since I wrote about sharing with the three atheists. The following day, nine good men came to my house and prayed for and with me. Thanks, Kevin, David, Wil, Kirk, Rod, Charlie, Steve, Robert, and Scott. Father, Your hand touched each of us that day. Thanks for Your healing balm. Your presence was intense, and I pray each man will live life hourly seeking You in all they do. Thank You.

Also this week, Cindy and I, with great anguish, acknowledged our weaknesses in our marriage. I confessed my not being the leader for Christ in our household. I ask, Lord, that You will help me to be the father and husband You want me to be. Help me to see the paths You are preparing for each of my family members and allow me to only be Your instrument in my role as dad, husband, and brother in Christ. Help me put aside my selfish desires and thoughts. Help me to encourage them to follow You.

I have been richly blessed, Lord. Praise to You. Thank You, Lord Jesus. Amen.

Chapter 41

Renewing the Mind

November 16, 2010

> *I had an appointment with my electrophysiologist today. He informed me that I have had only two runs of V tach over the last two and a half weeks since getting out of the hospital. Praise to God. Can you believe it? I had ventricular tachycardia twice, and I consider it a wonderful development. My ICD ATPed both occurrences while I was sleeping. I've noticed I'm not walking on eggshells as much these days and am finally starting to relax.*
>
> *"Therefore confess your sins to each other and pray for each other so that you may be healed. The prayer of a righteous man is powerful and effective" (James 5:16).*
>
> *I read in Adrian Roger's book, **What Every Christian Ought to Know Day by Day** (B&H, 2007), that faith is "my acceptance of God's acceptance of me." It has taken me **so long** to accept that God takes me **as I am**.*

For years, my orientation to the world hindered me greatly in my spiritual and psychological journey. Did you ever hear the joke by Groucho Marx? "I won't belong to any organization that would have me as a member." Unfortunately, I felt this way about many things, even being a member of heaven.

Where does this type of thinking originate? Certainly it is not of God.

Maybe it dates back to my childhood. My dad, when trying something new like food at a restaurant or a new tool would always say, "You know what would make this even better?" Now apply that approach to a kid's life with whatever activity he or she is involved in. Each time the child hears, "You know what you could have done a little better?" or "Did you see what that other kid did?" he or she gets the message that his or her performance needs to be a little better.

When I went through college, I made excellent grades in chemical engineering and was president of the engineering honor society, Tau Beta Pi, accomplishments that most would have been pleased with. But not me. I became disenchanted with the school's quality since I did well there. So by the time I left college for medical school, I had no real sense of accomplishment. This way of thinking, which was extremely selfish and self-centered, bound and hindered my growth in my relationship with Christ, for it was difficult for me to understand why God would want someone like me. Along with the unfortunate event with my college girlfriend, I was well on my way to letting Satan talk me out of any relationship I had with Christ. I was on a path to destruction.

This approach to life made me wonder if I could ever join a club and be satisfied. I wanted a club of which I would be proud of my association. Finally, the pinnacle club, for this *Marcus Welby, MD*-watching youngster of the seventies, came along—medical school! Certainly being a member of *that* noble profession would break my dark shadow of pessimism and longing.

I remember all too well the puzzled look on my father's face when I told him I had been accepted to medical school, as if he were thinking, *You can't do that.* **Other** *kids do that.* He literally couldn't believe it and didn't believe it until I showed him the acceptance letter. After he read the letter, instead of congratulating me, he just looked at me with disbelief, apparently wondering how in the world his offspring could pull off something like this. You see, I didn't belong in "that club" (medical school) according to my dad, who believed if you didn't belong, you have no business being there. In the following months, I received letters from my dad, telling me what the starting salary was for a chemical engineer. He just didn't know my desire or passion.

Four years later, I finally felt a sense of accomplishment when I walked across the stage during graduation from medical school, a fulfilling day for me. I stood a little taller and spoke with more authority. Humble and grateful I was not. I had accepted Christ when I was seventeen, but I was still struggling with the same old battles year-in, year-out. I finally had accomplished something I was proud of, and I did it *on my own,* or so I thought. I had forgotten the nights dreaming about the opportunity and making deals with God that, if given the chance, I would consider the mission field or anything else He desired of me. My sense of self-accomplishment, however, erased any memory of my seeking God's involvement for getting me there. The arduous work of medical training that ensued continued to take its toll on my spiritual life, which would take years to recover.

Today, I realize God's kingdom isn't a club that requires a resume of my previous successes or accomplishments. I also don't discredit it because I *get* to be a member like I did with my college. The difference this time is *I didn't earn* this membership, and its merit isn't based on *my* capabilities or how hard *I* worked. This time, I was *invited* to join, just as I am, and I responded to the invitation because I believe there is nothing more loving, pure, truthful, and forgiving than the gospel of Jesus Christ. He truly is the only path to God's heavenly kingdom. Christ fulfilled all the prophecies and promises from the Old Testament. His life on Earth was sinless; His teachings were flawless. And believing in His sacrifice leads to eternal life. Roman leaders couldn't find any guilt in Him to warrant His crucifixion, yet He still had to endure its pain and suffering. His "guiltless" death resulted in a sacrifice for the sin of all mankind. I am thankful for the opportunity to respond in the past, and I look forward to my life with this renewed spirit. Thank You, Lord Jesus. Amen.

Chapter 42

Faith, Hope, and Grace

November 17, 2010

Oh that my spirit's desire would supersede any desire that longs for something of this world.

Earthly pleasures are temporary and numb the spirit in me. Instead of the episodic and ecstatic fulfillment of earthly pleasures, I am left longing for something that heals and is long-lasting. These things are related to God and His timing. I don't want to wait, for I feel I need so much now, but practicing the spiritual disciplines of prayer, Bible study, worship with other Christians, and service will help me to develop the patience required to see God work in my life.

November 20, 2010

Yesterday, I went to a "lament" that a friend and his wife were having at their home in remembrance of their sixteen-year-old son who had committed suicide a year earlier on that date. I wasn't sure how intense the situation was going to be, but I felt God led me there to encourage and console them.

I met a very loving man named Pete who had been diagnosed with multiple myeloma eight months earlier and who is now in remission. He had to have a stem cell transplant along with chemotherapy. He felt horrible during his therapies and thought that he might die sooner than expected. We shared the similar thoughts we both developed during our struggle with our respective serious illnesses as well as our need to live each day more in the moment. We talked about our fear and the need to be reassured by God's presence. I shared my stories with him, but I must share one he told me (with Pete's permission).

"I was in the hospital and had a sleepless night before my stem cell transplant. I was discouraged and felt abandoned by God, yet I continued to seek His assurance like never before. God came to me in prayer that night and reassured me he had not abandoned me. He told me, 'You won't see me working in the big things for quite sometime, so I want you to look for me in the little things.' A few moments later, three nurses stepped into my room—a chemotherapy nurse, a regular floor nurse, and another nurse with the transplant team. The three supposedly had never worked as a team before. They introduced themselves as Faith, Hope, and Grace (their **real names**). It was as if the Lord had winked at me. I smiled and my heart winked right back."

My new friend certainly received the reassurance he needed that day. I love how his story illustrates that God is always present, listening to and acting on our prayers. His actions aren't always as obvious as my new friend's experience, but His timing of when and how to respond to our prayers is always perfect. I am thankful He knows my thoughts and needs before I ever verbalize them, yet He still wants me to ask. His answers to my prayers bring such contentment and reassurance.

As Christians, I feel we need to encourage one another with our stories of God working in our lives—not to boast but to remind one another of His active participation in our lives and that He is with us now.

His Spirit desires our attention. I freely give Him mine today. Thank You. Amen.

Chapter 43

Glimpses of Heaven

November 21, 2010

> *I drove through the Texas Hill Country heading west on State High-*
> *way 46 during the late afternoon yesterday—the time of day when*
> *the sunlight casts a brilliant yellow haze across the rolling hills ac-*
> *companied by extending shadows from the majestic oak trees that*
> *line the fields and roadways. The native grasses stand about one and*
> *a half feet tall this time of year and look like golden waves of wheat*
> *as they sway with each zephyr passing through. I was listening to a*
> *Handel piece for cello and piano as I drove, surrounded by God's cre-*
> *ation of which I am a part. I truly appreciated the moment.*

I remember a similar feeling twenty-four years ago while flying in a "46," a double-bladed navy helicopter, over the Indian Ocean. I was often transported from ship to ship by one of these large vertical flying machines while serving as a medical officer with Destroyer Squadron Seven (ComDesRon 7), as I provided emergent or routine medical care to the sailors on the support ships that included frigates, destroyers, and supply ships. These ships were accompanying the aircraft carrier USS *Ranger* and the battleship USS *Missouri* for protection, if needed.

It had been an extremely long day, and I was bushed. I had been out to sea for over forty days as the battle group prepared for future operations, which included going through the Strait of Hormuz to the Persian Gulf and bombing Iranian oil derricks. I had grown weary and stir crazy by the restricted space, constant noise, odors, and endless hum of activity aboard these floating industrial plants affectionately known as United States Navy warships.

It was a crystal clear afternoon, leading toward dusk—about the same time of day as my car trip. I hopped a ride on the helicopter to the aircraft carrier and happened to be the only passenger aboard other than the flight crew. I took my usual seat, latched myself in, and sat back. We had to fly quite a long distance that day, so the pilot took us to a much higher elevation than any of my previous helicopter rides. As we climbed, one of the flight crew asked if I wanted to sit by the large opening on the side of the helicopter where I could let my legs hang over the side and catch a better view. "Sure" I said. The crew member must have known something about riding at that time of day and its effect on a person's soul, for I *needed* a better view that day.

As I sat seemingly all by myself, hearing only the rhythmic beating of the rotors and gazing upon the vast ocean below and the endless sky above, I experienced one of the most peaceful, rejuvenating, and tranquil moments of my life.

When I receive a unique opportunity to witness God's creation in an intimate way, I always feel refreshed and rejuvenated, for it gives me a glimpse into His kingdom and *restores my soul*.

> *He makes me lie down in green pastures, he leads me beside quiet waters, he restores my soul. (Psalm 23:2-3)*

Chapter 44

The Weight Room

November 22, 2010

> *In this you greatly rejoice, though now for a little while you may have had to suffer grief in all kinds of trials. These have come so that your faith (of greater worth than gold, which perishes even though refined by fire) may be proved genuine and result in praise, glory, and honor when Jesus Christ is revealed. (1 Peter 1:6–7)*

The weight room at the YMCA is filled with various machines to challenge my strength, dexterity, and determination. With a coach and proper approach, I can become stronger, more agile, and increasingly assured about what my body can do. Each station stresses areas of my body that haven't been developed. A good coach looks at balance, watches for fatigue, and knows when and how to deliver the proper resistance without injuring the body.

So it goes with my faith and in utilizing my strength coach—God. During challenging trials (workouts), He applies stress, or pressure, at the proper time to help develop my faith so I can be increasingly more affirmed, steadfast, loving, and joyful in my life. My faith grows, and my endurance to run the race increases as I persevere and listen to my Coach with confidence that He will never lead me astray or let me down. He satisfies me in ways that far exceed anything I can obtain on this planet by myself.

This process of being refined as I am tested through trials helps me to develop godly characteristics, or fruits of the spirit: love, joy, peace, patience, kindness, goodness, faithfulness, gentleness, and self-control. God continues to mold me with His gentle hands, and like the potter who never lifts his hands from his vessel; I know my Potter never lifts His hands from me.

Thank You, God. Amen.

> *For you have been born again, not of perishable seed, but of imperishable, through the living and enduring word of God. (1 Peter 1:23)*

> *Therefore be clear-minded and self-controlled so that you can pray. (1 Peter 4:7)*

November 24, 2010

> *Therefore, since Christ suffered in His body, arm yourselves also with the same attitude, because he who has suffered in his body is done with sin. As a result, he does not live the rest of His earthly life for evil human desires, but rather for the will of God. (1 Peter 4:1–2)*

> *For this very reason, make every effort to add to your faith goodness; and to goodness, knowledge; and to knowledge, self-control; and to self-control, perseverance; and to perseverance, godliness; and to godliness, brotherly kindness; and to brotherly kindness, love. For if you possess these qualities in increasing measure, they will keep you from being ineffective and unproductive in your knowledge of our Lord Jesus Christ. (2 Peter 1:5–8)*

Chapter 45

Thanksgiving

November 25, 2010

> *He has made everything beautiful in its time. He has also set eternity in the hearts of men; yet they cannot fathom what God has done from beginning to end. (Ecclesiastes 3:11)*

> *They overcame him by the blood of the lamb and by the word of their testimony; they did not love their lives so much as to shrink from death. (Genesis 12:11)*

November 27, 2010

> *My hope is I will develop a more realistic view of heaven. I want my life to be peaceful with respect to death, including its cause and timing. I want my regained assurance of Christ in me to continue to influence my greater understanding of my eternal identity.*

December 6, 2010

> *As I grow hungry and Satan tempts me with various ways to satisfy my hunger, I pray I will remain steadfast for Christ and His teachings and only thirst for His refreshing water and hunger for His bountiful plenty. I want to tell Satan to just leave. Life on Earth is a battle and a journey. I pray my mind will expand from the here and now*

and begin considering eternity. May my actions on this earth point to Christ. Thank You, Jesus, through the Holy Spirit. Amen.

Later ...

*Why do I think I deserve such fulfillment while on Earth? Yes, I have joy, but am I so miscalculating as to think I will never need to deal with what this world offers daily? Trials, temptations, and struggles I know I will see. But I am surrounded by His love and beauty in the hearts of those who love Him and believe in Him. Can I be patient enough to live only for those things that are of Him during my short time on Earth, knowing there are much greater things to come? Do I believe in those things of which I write? Father, give me faith and hope of being with You in eternity. Help me to understand that my fullest life exists when I am most empty of the things of this world. Like John Eldredge states in his book **Desire**, "Enjoy the glass of cabernet, but drinking the whole bottle is another thing." Dear Lord, help me to understand moderation, and forgive me when I have overindulged and have deafened and numbed myself to Your voice and touch. Please take away those things that hinder my relationship with You. May my heart always be exposed to Christ, and may I not live to please only my desires. Praise to the King. Amen.*

December 11, 2010

I fear forgetting. Some of the Jews forgot the parting of the Red Sea as they escaped Egypt and Pharaoh, their safety during the Passover, and the daily manna from heaven as they wandered in the desert for forty years. Many complained about their condition, even saying they preferred slavery in Egypt again. How do I avoid such shortsightedness? How do I remember the goodness and love shown me during my trials throughout my life? To know His presence always is something I desire and seek.

December 15, 2010

Cindy shared a verse with me today.

Brothers, I do not consider myself yet to have taken hold of it, but one thing I do: Forgetting what is behind and straining toward what is ahead, I press on toward the goal to win the prize for which God has called me heavenward in Christ Jesus. (Philippians 3:13–14)

But our citizenship is in heaven. And we eagerly await a savior from there, the Lord Jesus Christ, who, by the power that enables him to bring everything under His control, will transform our lowly bodies so that they will be like His glorious body. (Philippians 3:20–21)

IV. A New View

Chapter 46

Turning the Corner

December 16, 2010

*I'm back in Cleveland today for reevaluation. Cindy and I arrived yesterday on the heels of a severe blizzard that blanketed the city with two feet of fresh snow. Cindy and I were thankful we made it here with **no** delays. God continues to have us wrapped in His arms. I discovered I haven't had V tach (not even short, non-sustained V tach) for **six weeks**, which makes me feel **really great**. I am not walking on eggshells any more, and my ability to relax has grown significantly. It was great walking through the airport, and not requiring a wheelchair. I look forward to what God wants to show me today through the PET scan.*

*"So that by His death he might destroy him who holds the power of death—that is, the devil—and free those who all their lives were held in slavery by their **fear of death**" (Hebrews 2:14–15, emphasis added).*

Do I fear death any more? I so feared death in May of this year after my first V tach episode. Only my faith in Jesus frees me from slavery to the "fear of death."

December 17, 2010

Cindy and I had dinner with Pastor Goode and his wife last night at our hotel in Cleveland. It was fun talking to and sharing with them my experience at their church (Euclid Avenue Church of God) on October 10. Both are godly folks with children of similar ages as ours. Christians sharing their experiences with one another is encouraging, enlightening, and edifying.

December 23, 2010

I finally received my PET scan results from the sarcoidosis specialist in Cleveland yesterday. I am very pleased about the changes. The lung, lymph nodes, and right side of my heart illustrate no FDG uptake (no inflammation). The left ventricle has significant scarring and still has twelve-percent active sarcoid (down from thirty percent in October)—a definite improvement, although the specialist wanted to see less than six percent. Treatment decisions are empiric and totally based on my current clinical conditions, side effects to meds, and what the physicians feel comfortable with. It's very much a balancing act, as there are no treatment protocols, for there are no significant studies on this disease when it affects the heart. I keep hearing about "this patient" or "that patient" from the docs but a "series of patients" just doesn't exist. I'm totally at a point where each decision is made visit-by-visit by the various doctors.

The following is a an example of one of my visits (conversations) with a physician:

Doctor: We'll decrease the amiodarone to four hundred mg/day for one week. It takes a couple of weeks for the new dosage to reach its steady state. Hopefully no increases in the ectopy will result from the reduced dosage.
Me: The effects of the amiodarone on my vision are quite noticeable now. It's beginning to become very difficult to drive at night.
Doctor: That probably won't get better. We want you to stay on prednisone at sixty mg for another three weeks and then decrease to forty mg/day.
Me: I can only imagine how puffed up I am going to get.
Doctor: Your methotrexate dosage will be increased to fifteen mg/week, and we prefer it be given over two days and subcutaneously (SQ). Supposedly, the drug gets better absorption and decreased side effects when given SQ, according to the British literature. I'm considering drugs like

Humera and Remicade if we don't see improvement with the methotrexate. There were two cardiac sarcoid patients who received cardiac transplants recently.
Me (thinking to myself): Boy, I'm encouraged.

The conversations with doctors are sometimes so mechanical and sterile, but I never let that displace their sincere dedication, concern, and desire to help me. My doctors are great, with a capital G. This medical process warrants conversations like the one above at times, but I don't mind. My docs who are so hurried in the clinic are the ones who come to my bedside between eight and ten o'clock at night during my hospitalizations after they have worked an entire day.

Emergencies and delays happen in the medical world. When I am waiting on a physician who is an hour late, I no longer get upset. I know from previous hospitalizations and clinic visits that his greatest concern is the health of each of his patients. When I take myself out of the equation and concentrate on what God is providing, I can be patient all day. The physician isn't delaying my visit because I've been bad or because he doesn't want to take care of me. He is delayed because ... well, he is delayed. He will take care of me when he can. Patients tap their feet and throw verbal jabs at physicians when they think they are being overlooked or deserve better. Sounds a lot like Naaman to me.

My heart and mind were beginning to recover from being broken down the past eight months physically and for years spiritually. I was only beginning to truly understand the life I *thought* I had in Christ and now *knew* I lived in an eternal kingdom and had already passed from death into life.

My two hearts were responding to the medications and the prayers. Their weaknesses and irregular beats were fading for the first time in what seemed like forever. My earthly body was being transformed into a healthier specimen, yet I still knew I had quite a way to go. And my spiritual being had never felt so alive and free. "I am improving!" I wanted to proclaim to everyone, but I didn't have to say a word. Cindy and others could see that much more than a regular heartbeat was resurrecting my life, as there was now evidence that a whole new heart was responsible for every beat. My spirit was soaring!

Chapter 47

Enjoying Others' Journeys

December 27, 2010

*I felt and observed God working in my life today. I read and was en-
couraged by Psalm 143:5–6,*

> *I remember the days of long ago:*
> *I meditate on all Your works*
> *And consider what Your hands have done.*
> *I spread out my hands to You;*
> *My soul thirsts for You like a parched land.*

*When I awoke this morning, I thought about my day and prayed for
His presence and to guide me in all my ways.*

December 29, 2010

*We had dinner tonight with friends at a Cajun restaurant in Marble
Falls, Texas. The building is owned by a local church, although you
wouldn't have known it by its commercial appearance and location
on a busy street. Church members manage all aspects of the restaurant and most are Hurricane Katrina victims who were transplanted
in this area. Their church is named (and you won't believe this) The
Smok'n for Jesus Church, referring to Revelations 3:16 in which God
describes spewing us from His mouth if we are lukewarm. The res-*

taurant staff/church members wanted us to know they were neither cold nor lukewarm, but **hot**, and that is what causes the **"smok'n'."** We had a great meal, and Cindy and I were blessed by our waitress's story. I look forward to seeing her in heaven some day. I pray I am not lukewarm in God's sight anymore. I, too, want to be "red hot" and "smok'n" for Jesus!

> "Those whom I love I rebuke and discipline. So be earnest and repent. Here I am! Behold, I stand at the door and knock. If anyone hears my voice and opens the door, I will come in and eat with him, and he with me" (Revelation 3:19–20, emphasis added).

Thank You, Lord! Amen.

January 8, 2011

> And so we know and rely on the love God has for us. God is love. Whoever lives in love lives in God; and God in him. In this way, love is made complete among us so that we will have confidence on the day of judgment, because in this world we are like him. There is no fear in love. But perfect love drives out fear, because fear has to do with punishment. The one who fears is not made perfect in love. (1 John 4:16-18)

I think of the fear I had back on May 6, the day after my first episode of V tach and the day of my cardiac cath. I know I feared punishment for my sinful life, and that leaving this world might not be so great for me. I also feared leaving my family. But the past few months God has given me ample opportunity to see and hear of His love for me and also what it means to be a disciple of Christ. I crave His presence and regret any time I turned away from Him. I seek love and to love others. My desire to sin has waned, and I acknowledge the Holy Spirit's presence within me daily. His revealing Himself to me in so many ways illustrates His presence in my heart and life. I can **assuredly** now approach judgment day with no fear only because I know Christ lives in me. Amen.

> This is the confidence we have in approaching God: that if we ask anything according to his will, he hears us. And if we know

*that he hears us, whatever we ask, we know that we have
what we asked of him. (1 John 5:14-15)*

January 11, 2011

7:00 a.m.

*Because the one who is in you is greater than the one who is in
the world. (1 John 4:4)*

*If anyone has material possessions and sees his brother in need
but has no pity on him, how can the love of God be in him?
Dear children, let us not love with words or tongue, but with
actions and in truth. (1 John 3:17)*

*If our hearts do not condemn us, we have confidence before
God and receive from Him anything we ask because we obey
His commands and do what pleases Him. And this is His
command: To believe in the name of His son, Jesus Christ, and
to love one another as He commanded us. (1 John 3:21)*

January 14, 2011

*My physical heart is improving and although I am limited in my ac-
tivity, I at least am not having bouts of V tach. Cindy can see that I
have a more relaxed look on my face these days. She said, "Last fall,
you were humped over with a very concerned, continuous stare." I've
started whistling again, and she said, "That had gone away too."*

*God has provided me an opportunity to serve Him on this earth. One
of the services is to love Cindy as Christ loved the church. Christ died
for the church. He gave up **everything** for it. I similarly need to learn
what this means for Cindy. My different expressions of that love
needs to be my priority in the days ahead. The fruits of the spirit I
hope will someday be evident in my life. I am finally at a point where
my daily thoughts aren't directly related to my illness but are related
to **my life**. I can't worry any longer about each atypical heartbeat,
future procedures related to my ICD/ pacemaker/leads (wires), or
when the sarcoid might flare up again. I need to look at today, use it
for His glory, and acknowledge Him in all things.*

I discussed my status with Morgen and Wil and am so impressed by their maturity and empathy. I pray they will continue to mature in Christ and develop a disciplined lifestyle that will help them on their own journeys.

Yesterday was quite a day. In the morning, I went to Bear Moon and sat with Grover, Arthur, and Vern (the most unlikely trio one could ever imagine). Two ladies walked in whom I thought I recognized. As I was leaving, I introduced myself and realized it was my former neighbors (May and Megan) from Fair Oaks Ranch. They both shared with me their lives over the past year. I was amazed by what I heard.

Megan had spent ten months hospitalized after a major car wreck (MVA). She sustained a severe closed-head injury, multiple broken bones, splenectomy, and a partial intestinal resection. I had heard about a horrible accident months ago in front of Boerne's Walmart where one of the passengers had to be airlifted by helicopter to a trauma hospital in San Antonio, but I had no idea it was Megan.

May shared that her husband, Dwight, had died last year. She also had two close relatives and a dear, long-time friend die in the last three months. They openly discussed how God was active in their lives and how their faith was helping them through the trials. I was richly blessed by their testimonies.

January 30, 2011

I am preparing the benedictory prayer for Morgen's upcoming graduation from Geneva. This will be Geneva's first graduation. We have waited twelve years for this day. I can't wait. A few months ago, I wasn't sure I was going to make it to this event. I'm very thankful and honored to be asked to speak. I want the prayer to be Christ speaking through me by the Holy Spirit.

Chapter 48

Feeling Alive Again

February 2, 2011

> *"Acknowledge Christ to others and He will acknowledge you before God on judgment day" (Matthew 10:32).*

February 18, 2011

> *At times, I've noticed that the intensity of my seeking God has diminished as I have improved. I do not want my faith to be based on fear of death but on my understanding of who Christ is, why He came, and the redemption I will receive on the day of judgment because of my faith in Him. I definitely believe God will judge me someday, and I must say, it is not comforting to think about. But my fear of that day is gone.*

February 27, 2011

> *"...**His love endures forever.**" (Psalm 136, phrase is included in every verse)*

March 2, 2011

> *This has been quite a week. I found out last week that I am extremely hypothyroid (low thyroid), caused by the drug amiodarone. It is a*

nasty drug. I was started on Armor Thyroid, and the edema, severe fatigue, and paresthesias (numbness in oral cavity, hands, and feet) are dissipating. I knew I felt horrible, for I was often going to bed around seven or eight o'clock each evening. Now I have a much better understanding of patients who suffer from this problem.

I saw my electrophysiologist in San Antonio yesterday. He downloaded my ICD/pacemaker data. Hurray! While still completely dependent on my pacemaker, I have had no V tach episodes since November 10! They were all smiles at the clinic. He even wants me to decrease my dosage of amiodarone to two hundred mg/day. Great day!

March 20, 2011

It's a beautiful spring day on the front porch. I worked this week at my Boerne clinic by myself for the first time since August 12! It's been seven long months.

The doctoring was like riding a bicycle, but I was glad it was a slow day as I adjusted to the pace. I worked six hours after getting up at 6:30 a.m. and was exhausted toward the end of the shift. For a guy who used to work fourteen to fifteen twelve-hour shifts a month, including night and day shifts in a busy ER, it is pretty difficult accepting my now limited capacity. I hope with time my fatigue will improve, but it was invigorating and humbling to be able to see patients again. Thank You, Lord!

God has revealed His ability to overcome obstacles in my life. When I can't tolerate any more and think I am on the brink of destruction, God shows me a way out. He allows me to experience and see what He wishes for me to see in order for me to mature and grow in wisdom. These trials never cease, and my making it through one big trial doesn't reduce the likelihood of another one occurring. Each trial helps me to be better equipped for the next, but trials themselves do not produce change in me. It is the praying and searching during the trials and the resultant answers from God that encourage and ultimately bring about change in me. If it takes trials to get me to pray and search, I welcome each one of them until I learn to pray without them.

Today, I continue to praise God and acknowledge Him in everything. I attempt to identify worthless idols that leave me feeling incomplete. I freely give You my money, job, house, and possessions, Lord. May I have the wisdom and ability to not make them the ultimate objects I worship. Give me the insight to recognize any addiction I may have to such things. I pray that my desire to do as I please on this earth will never transcend my desire to serve You and to go wherever You desire me to go. This is not easy, but I will persevere in letting God have my mind, heart, spirit, and strength. Thank You, Lord. Amen.

March 28, 2011

> *For I am the LORD your God, who takes hold of your right hand and says to you, "Do not fear; I will help you." (Isaiah 41:13)*

> *The LORD is the everlasting God, the creator of the ends of the earth. He will not grow tired or weary, and His understanding no one can fathom. He gives strength to the weary, and increases the power of the weak. Even youths grow tired and weary, and young men stumble and fall; but those who hope in the LORD will renew their strength. They will soar on wings like eagles; they will run and not grow weary, they will walk and not be faint. (Isaiah 40:28–31)*

April 20, 2011

I began writing a book yesterday about my experience. May it bring God glory and point readers, Christian and non-Christian, to Christ. May all its thoughts come from God. May any notoriety be directed to God. My story is one of assurance, for once you commit your life to Christ, He will not let go or ever leave.

May 1, 2011

A.M.

I am four days away from my one-year anniversary of when I was first diagnosed with V tach. May 5. Cinco de Mayo. I thought I might never see this day, but here I am, ticking steadily away. God has brought me through trials; caused me to get my house, family, and business organized; and made me keenly aware of the importance of each daily activity in which I get to participate. He has allowed me to do things and make decisions I never thought I would have had the opportunity to do or make. God has opened my heart and revealed the mess I allowed to enter. He reassured me of His presence and of my need to be dependent on Him in all things.

Today, I will proclaim that God's mercies far outweigh the sins of this world. They certainly outweigh mine. My sins are confessed and forgiven. The consequences of those sins I can and must live with, but the joy I have because of Christ will forever shine brighter and will never be taken from me. I strive to do His will as He reveals it to me and will strive to keep my heart, mind, and soul responsive to Him. I will continue to confess my sins but not hold on to their decay. I am the Lord's child and in constant need of His discipline, correction, and encouragement in all areas of my life. I am assured of my faith and His presence in my life, and while I might get nervous in the future, I will not fear!

In His name,

Amen.

Chapter 49

Commencement: A New Beginning

May 15, 2011

I passed my one-year, V-tach anniversary and am continuing to improve. I have come a long way. I am thankful for God's tenderness through this process and acknowledge His presence and His working in my life through it all. I remember Pastor Goode's sermon, "A Condition of Your Hearts," in October and how that worship service reassured me of God's presence in my life and revealed the immense spiritual heart disease I had developed over the years. My physical and spiritual hearts are being treated simultaneously, and their potential prognoses are similar: either life or death. I am feeling stronger these days. My hearts are healing!

I am preparing my notes for the closing comments and prayer for the graduation ceremony at Geneva next Saturday. What a culmination of emotions, dreams, and outright joy during this reflective week. I praise God for the joy He brings when we are faithful to His Word.
I know victory is mine today, not because of my physical improvement, but because God has been with me, fighting to save my life in so many other ways!

Thank You, Amen.

Closing Remarks/ Prayer to Class of 2011
Geneva School of Boerne
May 21, 2011

Wow. The view is incredible from up here. You know, it is surprising what God can do through a social worker, homebuilder, teacher, bond trader, physician, and statistician. All of us are very thankful. Before Geneva was ever an idea, it was a plan. God's plan. He created, developed, and grew Geneva into what it is today. You see, God is the true founder of Geneva, and we are all part of His plan.

I look into the faces of this crowd today and see the history of Geneva, whether you've been here from the very beginning or just this past year. We all have stories of how God has used Geneva to change our child's life, but we never knew how much He would use it to change *our* lives.

Class of 2011, it's said you cannot experience victory without a battle. Through the years, both your class and Geneva have had your share of trials and battles, but the victories far outweigh the defeats, and one of those victories we celebrate today. Today, we get to witness what a Geneva graduate looks like, and I can tell you we are *very* satisfied! Class of 2011, I'd like to share a verse with you that has meant much to me this past year. I hope it will bring you encouragement in your days ahead.

> *He shall say:* "Hear, O Israel, today you *are going* into a battle against your enemies. Do not be faint-hearted or afraid. Do not be terrified *or give way* to panic *before them*. For the LORD your God is the one who goes with you to fight for you *against* your enemies to *give you victory.*" (Deuteronomy 20:3, emphases added)

Class of 2011, LIVE VICTORIOUSLY!

Prayer

Oh merciful God, whose mercies far outweigh the sins of this world, please forgive the sins of the one who speaks before you now.

Father, we are thankful You have revealed to us the only way to be righteous, and that is through the blood of the ultimate sacrifice, Jesus Christ.

We thank You for the ample provisions You have provided the Geneva School of Boerne these past twelve years. We lift up our arms and praise You, praise You alone. There is no one above Your name. You are the Redeemer, Savior, Abba, and the great I AM. We acknowledge our dependence on You.

Today, Lord, our hearts have no place for heartache. Your Spirit has filled our hearts with joy and thankfulness. We are in awe of the work You have done in the hearts of families, staff, and students.

Father, we ask You *to add faith* to these nineteen men and women of the Class of 2011 throughout their lives. Help them to be humble in spirit and mind so they may gain wisdom and knowledge. Father, You have taught them grammar, logic, and rhetoric according to Your worldview and have seen them use their bodies and minds to compete in academics, athletics, and the performing arts. We pray they have brought You honor and glory with their efforts.

This class has led Geneva through unchartered waters, and we have witnessed their cohesiveness, diversity, leadership, and commitment. Father, You tell us "Faith is being sure of what we hope for and certain of what we do not see." (Hebrews 11:1) The faith of these students and their parents I lift up to You now and ask for Your continued blessings.

Father, we raise a hand directed toward these nineteen graduates. We ask that by Your grace You pour Your blessings upon them like oil upon their heads, and let their cups overflow so they may have life and live it to the fullest. Help them to fear and acknowledge You in all things. Bless each one with mentors, teachers, and friends who will walk beside them on their path and offer encouragement and will lift them up in times of trial, and point them in the direction of the cross when they are searching. Embolden them with faith, and help each to grow in Christian maturity as they seek Your will for their lives. Help them be Christian leaders in their homes, workplaces, and churches in whatever country they may live.

Father, we give thanks for Your blessings to Geneva and ask you to continue to bless this school. May all who come in contact with Geneva know that the love of Christ reigns in the hearts of all who support, work, and attend to its campus. May Jesus Christ always be recognized as the founder, caretaker, headmaster, and visionary of the Geneva School of Boerne.

We give You thanks, Lord, and sing the words of David, "Not to us, oh LORD, not to us, but to Your name be the glory, because of Your love and faithfulness" (Psalm 115:1).

Father, we lift up our prayers in the precious name of our savior, Jesus Christ, and through the Holy Spirit. Amen.

May 25, 2011

I sit in the kitchen today, reflecting on the last few days since Morgen's graduation from Geneva. I am so proud of her and her classmates and know all of them will continue their lives based upon the firm foundation laid by God at Geneva. The commencement exercise was the most beautiful I have ever witnessed. From the bagpipes, the banners representing different "houses," the faculty in robes representing their own achievements to the speeches presented by students and former Secretary of State, the Honorable James Baker, all was such a blessing. Thank You, Lord.

Getting the chance to speak that day was humbling. My appearance has changed significantly since being on a high dose of prednisone. My face has significantly blown up like a balloon, and I can no longer button the top two buttons of my shirt.

My words were directed to the students and their families initially, but everything changed when I began to lift our thankfulness to God. Oh, what exhilaration I felt, knowing His presence was in that place and that all those attending knew He was the reason we were gathered. Tears of joy flowed from the eyes of each proud parent in the church that day. We celebrated with hearts filled with delight.

I hugged the other two couples whom Cindy and I had started the school with twelve years earlier. Thanks Joann, Paula, Bret, and Robert. I will never forget the look in your eyes. And to think the joy in heaven is so much more!

All of the founders know who is the true founder of Geneva, and we praised Him mightily. What a great day!

Chapter 50

Looking Forward to Tomorrow

June 5, 2011

*Cindy, Mo, Wil, and I are at Roddy Tree resort this weekend. We have been coming here every June for years now. We visit with other families from our town to relax, sing, eat, and hang out at the Guadalupe River. People come and go throughout the weekend, especially since the kids have gotten older with some now in college. It's always a fun few days, and this year for me it's very special. The beauty of my family and friend's faces is satisfying and enjoyable. All of this is **good.***

*I am reading Psalms from back to front. I don't know why I am reading it back to front, but I have enjoyed it immensely, especially the parts relating to the enormity and majesty of David's God. **My** God. David illustrates our God's awesomeness by referring to the nations, the heavens, and the earth. All very bold terms. Hearing such words daily is so refreshing. I will continue reading and look forward to His teaching.*

I have also been reading the book of Matthew about Christ performing miracles sometimes to prove His deity and other times as a response to people's faith in Him. I wonder if I was living then would I have scoffed at Him, or would I humble myself and kneel down before such a man? How would I have determined the deity of Christ?

Would my place in society have hardened me so that I would be fear-ful of what such a man would take away from me? (Matthew 9:34). Would I have thought that Christ "cast out demons" only because the "prince of demons" allowed Him to? Would I have understood how dependent I was on my place in life (or status) and have recog-nized the associated insecurity and spiritual blindness?

*Those who believed listened to His words and the depth of their meaning. They believed in the miracles and accepted that proph-ecy was being fulfilled. Their hearts were changed forever, and they allowed themselves to be filled by His love. They decided to follow Christ and forsake earthly (worldly) institutions and ways. They were given **faith**.*

*In my life, I have responded without seeing these things. I continue to receive faith in order to be certain of the things I have not seen. Given this, I tend to believe I would have responded to Christ then for the same reasons I respond now: my God-given faith and His **never-changing** message, love, and testament.*

Praise to God and all His holiness. Amen.

June 12, 2011

*I'm sitting on the front porch of my home drinking coffee while listening to the bells ringing from a nearby church. While I am yet not capable of running, I was able to walk two miles on a flat surface. Today is also the third day in a row I've appreciated no skipped beats in my heart. During my walk, I thought of how I was reading **Younger Next Year** a year and a half ago like it was my new bible, as exercise and fitness had become the most important things in my life after the pacemaker insertion. My perspective has changed considerably since then, and while I will continue to exercise the best I can, I will always keep the **true** gospel and the wonderful salvation it promises first in my heart.*

June 18, 2011

*It's Father's Day. What a great day! I was able to sit **in the bleachers** in 104-degree weather and watch Wil play two games of baseball. He hit a triple. My doing this was impossible last year when I could only* *watch from an air-conditioned car. Such changes have occurred this past year! I'm looking forward to tomorrow. Praise to God! Amen.*

June 28, 2011

> *I will say of the Lord, "He is my refuge and my fortress, my God, in whom I trust." (Psalm 91:2)*

> *Psalm 91 provides significant encouragement for those going through difficult times. Also, Matthew 12:36 reminds me that I am accountable for every careless word I speak.*

> *What joy I feel these days looking back at the past year: my illness and recovery, Geneva's first graduation and Morgen graduating in the same class, rejuvenation in my love for Cindy, a greater understanding of God in my life, and being able to walk two miles a day in the mornings when it is cool and now able to withstand one hundred-plus-degree temperatures at Wil's baseball games the last two weeks. Hallelujah!*

> *I go to Cleveland in two weeks. Whatever the results, I will praise God for the new life He has given me. I will acknowledge Him in all things. He is my refuge and my fortress.*

> *Praise to His glory. Amen.*

Fear of death obstructed my view of living when I was confronted with the reality of my heart disease. I have discovered that God takes the worry out of my life by eliminating the bondage to that fear. My perspective has changed as my "soul thirsts like a parched land." I rediscover my relationship to Christ each day as I learn to acknowledge Him in all things. His love endures forever, and my strength is renewed every day. He has expanded my view of life, which had been centered on the here and now. A much grander scale exposes His eternal kingdom, of which my time on Earth is but a portion. I am quite thankful for my new outlook that's revealed through the "spectacles" I now am wearing.

V. True Healing

Chapter 51

Adjustments

July 15, 2011

*I sat in the cardiologist's exam room in Cleveland today. I came by myself since I'm improving and Cindy feels okay with my traveling alone. As usual, I was initially seen by the pacemaker/defibrillator tech who connected my ICD wirelessly to his lap top computer and downloaded all my data. Afterward, he gathered the data and then changed the settings on my device with a click of a few buttons. I always hope he doesn't accidently miss a button. The changing of the settings on my device puts my ICD/pacemaker through various maneuvers and checks if my heart is beating on its own and whether any beats are conducted to the ventricles. I have been in third-degree AV heart block since that heralded day in May over a year ago and have been **totally dependent** on my pacemaker for every pulse in my arteries since.*

I felt my heart's rhythm bouncing around as he was going through the maneuvers. I was glad I had an experienced pacemaker tech, for the experienced ones always make sure I'm lying down during the procedure. They know that when cutting off the power to my pacemaker, the heart rate can slow considerably and I could become faint and potentially fall off the exam table.

*A funny thing was happening, though, for I wasn't getting dizzy or lightheaded this time. I noticed the tech appeared puzzled and played with the adjustments for a few additional minutes. He finally asked me, "How do you feel right now?" I answered, "Okay. I don't feel any different." He sat back in his chair and shook his head in disbelief. He happened to be a Christian, too, and I had shared my story with him. He cleared his throat and finally said, "Right now, your heart is generating beats on its own, and most of them are being conducted to your ventricles **unassisted** by the pacemaker—and all without any ventricular ectopy or irregularity!" I responded, "Excuse me, what did you say?" With an astonished look that matched mine, he repeated his answer. I questioned him, "How could this be? I have been in third-degree heart block for over a year now?" In all my years practicing medicine, I have never heard of anyone in third-degree heart block reversing spontaneously to a normal functioning electrical system a year later. We both looked at one another and then cried tears of joy. I loved being able to share that moment with a brother in Christ!*

I know many physicians can scientifically come up with explanations as to why my ability to conduct returned. Twenty-five percent of my left ventricle is scarred due to the sarcoidosis, so I figured the electrical system was too since it hadn't worked in over a year. Why did the tissue of the electrical system conduct beats again one year later?

I remembered my many fervent prayers that previous year, asking God to do with my heart as He pleased. For the first time, I think I finally *understood* He has the power to heal. His miracles of healing, as told in the New Testament, illustrated His deity and often were a response to someone's faith. I now have experienced His healing power. I have witnessed His mercy and grace. Thank You, Lord!

*After yielding my **spiritual** heart to God, I realized my complete dependence on Him. He became my "spiritual pacemaker." He "cardioverted" my spiritual heart to beat at **His** pace and to **His** rhythm. I never expected He would do the opposite with my physical heart, causing it to become independent of its pacemaker. I didn't realize I already had a cardiologist or heart specialist before ever visiting my first doctor in Boerne two years ago. The Great Physician knew my diagnosis all along and what I needed to be cured. He knew the course of therapy I had to endure. All He required of me was to trust*

Him. I have done my best and have experienced His treatment and now His cure.

In Cleveland that day, the cardiologist adjusted my pacemaker so my heart could beat more on its own. At my next cardiology checkup in San Antonio a couple of months later, the ICD illustrated I had previously been dependent on the pacemaker for over 99 percent of my beats, but after the adjustments in Cleveland, it had decreased to approximately 10 percent. I can't get over the number of adjustments I have received in so many ways during my trips to Cleveland this past year. God wanted me in Cleveland. And I am truly thankful.

In the future, whenever and wherever He leads, I will go.

September 14, 2011

> *"If the LORD delights in a man's way, He makes his steps firm; though he stumble, he will not fall, for the LORD upholds him with his hand" (Psalm 37:23–24).*

October 3, 2011

> *Lord, help me to see the world and its situations as You would have me see and not as I would want it and them to be. Thank You. Amen.*
>
> *Do my feet stand on level ground? Am I blameless?* ***Do I see myself as blameless before God?*** *Only through Christ's blood.*
>
> > *"My feet stand on level ground; in the great assembly I will praise the LORD" (Psalm 26:12).*
>
> *Amen.*

October 3, 2011

> *How do I become less of me and more of Christ? Whatever thought, idea, or vision I have, it cannot interfere with God's plan. I must be willing to stand firm for Christ, but issues in which I am standing firm for my sake only have got to diminish.*

Chapter 52

Death or "Just Leaving"

My conversation with God has clearly illustrated that I have both a physical and spiritual heart. Because of this fact and my better understanding of my relationship with God through Christ, I have reestablished my certainty in an eternal life—a life that includes my current earthly existence and a future time and place where my name is *already written*.

Death doesn't have the same grip on me like it once had through consuming fear and worry. The iceberg floating ominously in my hearts' seaward paths just months ago is now slowly melting away.

On November 12, 2011, I was given another chance to look at the issue of death, but this time it would be through a new set of spectacles.

November 12, 2011

> *Significant thoughts and situations related to death today. My father (age eighty-six) and sister-in-law (age forty-eight) will both start hospice care this week. My brother and sister are at my home, and we're having long discussions related to the end of life with its host of emotions and associated issues, and each person's response is shaded by their memories of the one who is dying. A friend approached Cindy and I two days ago with a prayer request regarding his dealing with the anniversary of his son's death that occurred two years ago. Another funeral of a good friend's dad was last week. Death and its grip on the world continue, but how, after what I have been through, do I perceive a "worldly death"*

now? Do I see it from God's perspective? What influences my re-
sponse? My answer revolves around these two things:

1. *The decisions I make illustrate my faith.*
2. *My decisions are dependent on my spiritual conditioning, which is based*
   on my God-given faith and the spiritual disciplines I practice daily.

I discovered my fear of death could only be conquered by faith in Jesus. So, the real question for me was, "Do I have faith in this Son of Man called Jesus the Christ?" Is it something I *know* mentally in my brain, or does my belief reach to the depths of my heart? Do I believe life *only* comes through Him (John 14:6–7; Romans 6:23)? Did He *alone* conquer death and demonstrate we all have freedom from Satan's grip (Romans 8:1–4)? The Bible tells me He returned three days after Calvary and displayed His scarred body to Mary, the two men on the road to Emmaus, His disciples, and others in various locations around Galilee. Was the purpose of this amazing death-defying act to provide a living sacrifice for all mankind? A sacrifice that atones for every man's sin? My sin (Romans 3:23–26)? *Believing* Jesus is the Son of God who was crucified, buried, and resurrected takes an act of faith (Hebrews 11:1). Faith in Christ grants *anyone* who is a sinner (that would be me and you) an opportunity to have a relationship with God while on this earth and throughout eternity (John 3:16). Do I believe all this is true? YES, I DO!

Since that day at the Euclid Avenue Church of God in Cleveland I have been assured of my faith in Christ and God's continued presence in my life. I know my faith transcends all fear associated with death and its earthly finality, sometimes painful process, and bodily decay. The decisions I make daily reflect who I am in Christ. My response to Christ's teachings and my faith in their inherent truth influences each decision I make. My path is easier to follow now as I listen to His guidance through the Holy Spirit. My focus is on pleasing my Father.

This godly trinity, which includes the Father, Jesus, and the Holy Spirit, was confusing to me when I first heard it explained at age seventeen, but understanding its importance became essential as I became a Christian. I have heard it explained using the following water analogy, and it made sense. I hope it helps you to understand too.

The analogy relates to the three different forms of water and how their properties describe the three members of the Trinity. H_2O comes in three forms: ice, liquid, and steam (vapor). Although different in form, they are always the same compound: two hydrogen atoms and one oxygen atom.

The liquid form when surrounding an object *completely* engulfs its surface, flows into every pore or crevice, and leaves no area untouched because of its *omnipresence*. This form represents the Father, who is omniscient and ever-present.

Ice has a hard, palpable surface at the junction between substance and air and stands erect. This would be Jesus, who walked with us and was composed of flesh and blood.

Finally, there is vapor, which is invisible to the human eye yet can be inhaled into the depths of our lungs with each respiration, reaching alveoli where elements cross membranes of the capillaries in our bloodstream. From there, elements are transported to every facet of our being. No site untouched. This form symbolizes the Holy Spirit, who dwells in our spirit after we acknowledge Christ as our Savior.

Each form expresses its own unique trait, yet all are the same. Christ and the Holy Spirit are extensions of the Father, but all are God.

This relationship with God the Father, God the Son, and God the Holy Spirit is my foundation for living daily. I cannot live any other way. Death has been conquered by Christ's sacrifice. Life is eternal for those who believe.

The permanence and finiteness of an earthly death is inescapable if the body with its inherent sinfulness is perceived as the only living entity on Earth. My physical body is meant to age, get stiff, and ultimately wear out like any other moving part created on this earth. Regardless of the number of adjustments my body receives to advance my years, I know one day it will still quit. My body does not have a warranty. None of them do, but I have discovered I have a *lifetime* guarantee on something that is more me than the "bag of bones" I now possess or the face people think of when they hear my name. That something is my spirit. A creature born not of this earth, but of somewhere else far removed. My spirit is a viable entity that is as real as the nose on my face and as unmistakable too. It extends eternally and longs for a place where heaven and Earth will be one someday. It is an alien or stranger on this earth (Hebrews 11:13–16) like those of the Old Testament figures Abraham, Isaiah, Daniel, David, and many others whose spirits desired a homeland not of this earth.

Someone may think, *Since I live on this planet, I must already have life. I mean, I am living a lifetime, aren't I?* My experience these past two years has taught me to say, "Not exactly," because for me, life's meaning has changed, and I can no longer truncate or limit its boundaries. Life exceeds the mechanical capability of our bodies and the intellectual prowess of a clear mind. *Life, living*, or being *alive* is eternal, everlasting and without end. This is how Christ transforms a being on Earth. He makes it *alive* (John 10:9–10)!

If life becomes eternal after acknowledging Christ as Savior and receiving the Holy Spirit, what actually occurs when my body stops functioning? What is that called? It can't be death, for death represents the end of life, and I have concluded that life must be eternal. Is it "the end?" Once again, no, based on the same argument. So what is it? I now believe that the moment my heart stops, my brainwaves are suspended, and my diaphragm gasps its last breath is the beginning of a transition, much like going from adolescence to adulthood or from an infant to a toddler. I don't remember if I knew exactly what transitioning from adolescence was going to look like, and I certainly didn't know what was coming next as an infant, but each transition was accompanied by wonderful discoveries that led to greater maturity. The things that scared me as a child no longer do. My current earthly phase will end. I don't fear what's next any more.

Does my physical, emotional, and psychological existence define my life? I no longer can adhere to this thinking either, for it doesn't make sense to me. God has revealed Himself to me in almost palpable measures this year. He has reassured me of my faith, and I continue to accept Him as my Savior based solely on my belief and nothing else. My spirit lives, of this I am sure, and will never decay. I am alive right now on this earth because of my spirit that resides within me. I didn't die last year because God was not ready for my spirit to leave this world or my "bag of bones." My spirit and I are one and the same. I used to only see a two-dimensional image when standing in front of a mirror, but no longer. My spirit is as much me as my pinky toe and is as real as the beating of my heart.

I read a poem entitled "Miss Me But Let Me Go" by Edgay Albert Guest that was presented at a funeral recently. The following specific lines stood out:

Why cry for a soul set free?...
...For this journey we all must take and each must go alone.
It's all part of the Master's plan, a step on the road to home.
Miss me a little, but let me go.

When my bodily journey ends and my spirit is set free, I hope a moment of inspiration will transpire for those who believe, for they know of my future with the saints, the Father, and the King. This earth is not the end of my trail by any means.

*An example of a Christian's physical death and journey to heaven is beautifully illustrated by J. R. R. Tolkien in his trilogy, **The Lord of the Rings (1955)**, which was adapted into three movies. In the* *third volume's film adaptation, **The Return of the King (2003)**, Bilbo Baggins, the elder hobbit, radiates great expectation as he boards the last ship to leave Middle Earth to begin yet another journey. This journey, however, will take him far away from the shire, never to return. His young friends are saddened by his departure, but Bilbo's mood is upbeat and filled with anticipation as he sails away for he knows of where he is going, yet still a mystery. He knew the time to leave the shire had come. No fear existed in his eyes.*

*Praise to our Father who uses each step of **life** for His glory. Even, our earthly death! Amen.*

Chapter 53

Clarity Through Unclear Lenses

Saved doesn't mean *no suffering*, it means *no death*.
   —Adrian Rogers, *What Every Christian Ought to Know Day by Day*

November 9, 2011

> *I visited my parents today at the New Hope Assisted Living Center. My dad is in hospice care now. His end is nearing. He can still converse, but his ability to understand and his memory are significantly eroding. I showed him old pictures. He seemed to enjoy them, though I'm not sure he knew who the people were in the pictures.*
>
> *During our limited conversation, he stopped abruptly and looked directly into my eyes. He stated with the surest look on his face, "You're going to be around awhile" and "You are the richest, and I mean in all the ways." I was so taken back by the **clarity** of the words from a demented man who doesn't remember my name and often tells me, "Say hi to your parents," every time I leave his room. The statements were so poignant. I couldn't help but think God was directly speaking to me. I will treasure these words forever.*

My dad's statement was reassuring, for "being around awhile" was soothing to hear after experiencing the events of the past two years. "The richest, and I mean in all the ways" made me feel perhaps he had recognized a change in the sincerity of my faith. I know my faith isn't richer than anyone else's, but his *acknowledgement* of witnessing *a change in me* was very special.

November 14, 2011

> *Don't be afraid.*

>> *"Faith is being sure in what you hope for and certain of what you cannot see" (Hebrews 11:1).*

November 15, 2011

> *He is the farthest away from me and the closest to me.*

>> *"I will not die but live, and will proclaim what the LORD has done. The LORD has chastened me severely, but He has not given me over to death" (Psalm 118:17).*

>> *"Give thanks to the LORD, for he is good; His love endures forever!" (Psalm 118:29).*

> *I have been thinking a lot about the "whats" of the world and the "hows." **What** I have is immaterial compared to **how** I got it. What job, what position, what level of education, what salary, what neighborhood I live in, etc. all fail in comparison to **how** I got the job or position, **how** I achieved my education or financial standing, or **how** I got to where I live. What I gain or achieve in this earthly life is well known by the world and is the standard by which I am judged, but God and I are the only ones who know how I got there. And His standard is all that matters. You see, how I got anywhere is an **eternal** thing. My boasting about **what** I have attained is no longer needed; my boasting about **how** God is molding my life and the resultant vessel is never stopping. Amen.*

Chapter 54

No Doubt

It had been over two years since I took that fateful jog down Main Street in June 2009. The journey had been arduous, yet invigorating; sorrowful, yet joyful; at times confusing, yet enlightening. I am forever grateful for the path and the conversations along the way.

My journey advanced through three phases, which coincide with the stages a patient travels during the medical and/or surgical management of disease: diagnosis, treatment, and recovery. The last phase, recovery, can lead to renewal or demise, depending on the correctness of diagnosis and the response to treatment. I was in the final phase of recovery in December 2011 and knew that genuine healing was occurring in both my hearts, as each was further away from the diseased path it was traveling. I was improving, but I wasn't quite finished yet, for I had one more visit to my electrophysiologist.

Dec 12, 2011

> *Today, I went to my **last** cardiology appointment. My electrophysiologist put me through an exercise treadmill test in his office located in Boerne to assess the dynamics of my heart and the ICD/pacemaker during exertion. I had asked him to do this, for I needed to know what physical potential I could strive for safely. I also needed to know what limits I would have to learn to live with. Previously this year, he told me I would never be able to run again. But since that day, I have continued to improve in unexpected ways, especially these last*

few months since my third trip to Cleveland. I can't help but wonder where God's healing might take me. My life has already shown that anything can happen when God is involved. I know I am no longer limited by the boundaries this world sets, and my hope rests in something that exists far outside the confines of this world.

I began the stress test strapped to multiple leads, two monitors, and a nurse taking my blood pressure every two minutes. Starting out, my heart rate was in the seventies, and it was paced. As I started huffing and puffing when walking a brisk pace, my heart rate increased to eighty, ninety, one hundred bpm. "How are you feeling?" my cardiologist asked. I said, "Okay," so he inclined the treadmill and sped it up. I saw 110, 115 bpm on the heart monitor. **I'm starting to sweat now**, I thought. **I'm not sure how far we should take this thing**.

The staff seemed tense, but my cardiologist was smiling, for he had noticed something. As my heart rate increased, my SA node had taken over and **every** electrical impulse generated was my own. Every beat was also being conducted to my right and left ventricles **without** the aid of my pacemaker wires, thus resulting in an all-organic, homemade heartbeat. In other words, the autopilot was off, and I was flying (beating) **totally on my own again**. I had at times required the pacemaker at lower rates since my last appointment in Cleveland in July, but my docs now thought that perhaps my dependence was caused by the settings of the pacemaker and not necessarily by my heart.

After a few adjustments to the pacemaker, I was soundly beating completely on my own with no palpitations. Life is like that it seems— a few adjustments and our "hearts" beat again as they should. As a physician, I thought I knew which adjustments were needed for correcting my heart problem. But little did I know which heart required the greatest evaluation and treatment. Fortunately, I had the Great Physician by my side the entire time who knew my real heart's disease, treatment, and cure.

My physical heart is now independent of the paced electrical beats from the Medtronic pacemaker located in my chest wall under the left clavicle. My spiritual heart, however, relies one hundred percent on the reassuring and never-ending jolts from my godly pacemaker, the Holy Spirit, which is deeply embedded in the depths of my soul (or clay). I have had enough with trying to control the beating of my spiritual heart. True **cardioversion** has finally occurred!

The clinic's third-story window in front of the treadmill allowed me to see the rolling hills surrounding Boerne for miles and miles. It was cloudy and cold, but I thought it was the most beautiful day of my life. While walking on the treadmill and gazing out the large window, I thought of my journey the past couple of years with the multiple V tach episodes, second- and third-degree AV heart blocks, three cardiac ablations, multiple hospitalizations, ICD/pacemaker placements, being defibrillated, and the drugs and their side effects. But I also remembered that day in May when I feared death and questioned my faith, the three verses I now recite daily before getting out of bed, my Bible study, quiet days spent at home conversing with God, Euclid Avenue Church of God, Pastor Goode, Ms. Betty Williams, and finally the night I witnessed Jesus smiling at me. I thought of where I had started and where I am now. I gave God thanks for bringing me to this place. I will never be the same.

I left the clinic and hopped into my car with a heart **continuously** beating **on its own** for the first time in two years—a heart that was incapable of conducting a single beat from the SA node to the ventricles one year ago. Its steady beat felt like a finely tuned engine humming synchronously in my chest; the bouncy, off-tilt washing machine, which I had grown accustomed to this past year, was now gone.

As I drove away from the clinic, my iPod was playing "Fix You" by Coldplay. This is what I heard: "Tears come streaming down your face. Lights will guide you home and ignite your bones, and I will try to fix you." My tears were streaming down my face. I do look forward to lights guiding me home someday, and with no doubt, **I know** Who fixed me.

Praise to You, Father. Amen.

> "I am telling you the truth: those who hear my words and believe in him who sent me have eternal life. They will not be judged, **but have already passed from death to life** (John 5:24, GNT, emphasis added).

Conclusion

Each of us at some point during our earthly existence needs advanced cardiac life support in the ICU of life. When that moment happens it usually occurs when we least expect it, yet when we need it most. The Great Physician approaches and sits at our bedside. He explains how serious our heart has deteriorated as we listen with quickened, anxious breaths for we are afraid of dying. We are at His mercy to do something miraculous, for we know we are running out of time. We ask Him to do *anything* before it's too late, and He offers us the *only cure* available: a heart transplant.

We are terrified by these words and recoil upon hearing them. We are fearful of stepping forward, for the distance toward the cure may be too far to leap. We fumble with our words and wonder how we got into this situation in the first place. *If I don't have the procedure, I will surely die*, we think to ourselves. *But if I have it and trust Him, I have a chance to live.* Finally, we say to the Great Physician, "I trust You," while looking into His compassionate eyes. "I will let You have my diseased, dying heart in exchange for a living, healthy one." He smiles and confirms our request. Suddenly, the nursing staff is scurrying about, wondering what is going on. All the monitors have returned to normal! The IV drips no longer are needed. Discharge orders have already been written. The "transplant" has *already* occurred! We can't believe it was that fast.

December 12, 2011, is the last journal entry I penned related to my cardiac experience. It did not end the conversation, however, for I continue to seek God daily with assurance and confidence, knowing I never lost my salvation and that I *already* live in His eternal kingdom. My journey on Earth carries on, but I know a fateful voyage someday (a date I cannot predict) will take me far away, and I won't return. When that day arrives, I will gaze confidently ahead with anticipation and not with the dread I felt on May 6, 2010. Sorrow in the hearts of those who wave good-bye to me will be temporary, for after I leave, they will know upon what I am gazing.

You are on a journey, too, perhaps with questions and fears similar to mine. If so, be assured of this: You will be all right. Be patient, and look for His grace. I encourage you to read John10:28; Romans 8:35; and Phillipians 1:6. Consider their message, and then *pray* and *seek* God.

Remember my analogy comparing Christian life to riding a bicycle? As

Christians (riders) pedal closer toward the cross their bikes become stronger, sturdier and more capable. We relinquish our handlebar grip to God and He begins to steer us where we *need* to go. At times He guides our course toward the edge of the path near the gnarly trees. He does this because He has witnessed our spiritual growth as evidenced by our running away from sin and avoiding idols that distract us from Him. We can almost touch the thorns, but He knows the temptation of the forest isn't as overwhelming as when we first began pedaling. He knows we now say, "Get away satan, I believe in the One who has already conquered your ways." While riding near the edge of the path our new orientation shifts our *focus* from the trees to something previously unnoticed: the multitude of people who have gathered at the path's edge. Some have bikes while others do not. With heads hung low those walking along side their bikes appear tired and weary. Their bikes appear worn with flat tires, broken chains, and marred paint. The riders have struggled through the dense forest resulting in hidden wounds that are illustrated by their torn, blood-stained clothing. Despair and a longing to return to the path is painted on their faces. They question how they lost their focus and why they left the path by jumping the curb.

The riders still on the path stop and offer to fix the flat tires and repair the broken chains. We help adjust the seat as we support their bikes upright. We encourage them to get onto their bike and pedal once again. We gently give them a push toward the middle of the path where they can more easily focus their gaze in the direction of the cross.

Others at the curb's edge are without bikes. We carefully, but purposefully, pull up next to them and share our story related to our own bike's journey and final destination. We encourage them to consider getting a bike of their own. We explain to them the bike is a gift from God and given according to His grace. Some respond to the invitation and others do not, but *everyone is invited* to ride. The rider's role is to share what he or she has been shown along his or her own path. We cannot, however, make others get on a bike. That is a *personal* choice between them and God.

I hope you enjoy "the ride" of your life. If you don't have a bike I hope you will consider getting one by asking God (It's as simple as acknowledging your sinfullness and separation from God, and then accepting Jesus Christ into your heart as your Lord and Savior). By God's grace this can happen to anyone. Once you are sitting atop your seat begin pedaling and stop *worrying* about your mistakes (or sins). You are going to make them. Hopefully, their frequency will decrease over time, but they will not totally disappear as you grow in your faith. Admit and confess them to your Father, and ask His forgiveness. Strive to improve (repent or turn away from your sin) before getting out of bed each day. Stay on your path, try to avoid the potholes, and let God take the handlebars. If you fall off, get up and start pedaling again. You are *still* on the path. Know you are loved by a gracious and merciful God who desires good things for you.

You will feel like you have let Him down at times, but remember, our Savior, Jesus Christ, has already gone to the Father and has hidden all our past and future blemishes from Him through the blood He shed on the cross. Take a deep breath, relax, and be confident that your heart is filled with the Holy Spirit. Ask Him to displace any worries, wrong thinking, hurt, or bitterness you may have.

Today, my physical heart beats strongly on its own with great regularity. Why and how I am not sure, but I am thankful. My spiritual heart, however, *never* beats on its own any more. Of that I *am* sure. Its beats are sustained *forever* by my holy pacemaker, a heavenly device implanted deeply within my heart years ago.

I have no doubt about my assurity in Christ now, and I am eternally grateful for His healing touch. All He requested of me was to desire and seek Him only, to acknowledge Him in all things, and to thank Him unceasingly. He has shown me the way back to the path, His hands are steering my bike's handlebars, and He has done it all by renewing the beating of my "hearts."

Thank You, Lord.

Very Much.

Appendixes

Heart Physical Therapy

How do you keep your heart in great shape? For your physical heart, you must exercise, see your doctor regularly, eat right, and monitor your cholesterol. Analogously, for your spiritual heart, you must practice the following spiritual disciplines:

Get a *Bible*, and *read* it regularly.
Pray daily.
Fellowship with other believers.
Serve.

Daily Reminders

These are thoughts and verses I have reviewed daily since May 6, 2010.

Jesus is Lord.
Christ died for me and conquered death by His resurrection. I am redeemed forever.
Christ has authority over heaven and earth.
I am valuable in God's eyes. (I do not seek acceptance from this world.)
Do I live for eternity?
What does my heart desire?
Remember to pay attention to those things that draw me closer to God.
Psalm 139:23–24
Deuteronomy 20:3
1 Corinthians 13:4

Live hourly!

The only thing that counts is faith expressing itself through love (Galatians 5:6).

Love the Lord your God with all your heart, soul, and mind (Deuteronomy 6:5).

Love your neighbor as yourself (Leviticus 19:18).

Sources

Berryman, Buckland, Martin, Champion. Fix You. X&Y. Parlophone Records, 2005.

Crosby, Fanny Jane, Knapp, Phoebe Palmer. Blessed Assurance. Public Domain, 1873.

Eldredge, John. Desire: The Journey We Must Take to Find the Life God Offers. Nashville: Thomas Nelson, 2000, 2007.

Keller, Timothy. The Prodigal God: Recovering the Heart of the Christian Faith. New York: The Penguin Group. 2008.

Keller, Timothy. Counterfeit Gods: The Empty Promises of Money, Sex, and Power, and the Only Hope That Matters. New York: The Penguin Group, Adult. 2009.

Lucado, Max. Fearless: Imagine Your Life Without Fear. Nashville: Thomas Nelson, 2009.

Rogers, Adrian. What Every Christian Ought to Know Day by Day: Essential Truths for Growing Your Faith. Nashville: B&H Publishing Group. 2007.

About the Author

Brian Fowler, MD, is a native Texan. He is board certified in emergency medicine and has treated over one hundred thousand patients. After serving eight-years in the United States Navy, he settled with his wife, Cindy, and their two children, Morgen and Wil, in the beautiful Texas Hill Country. He is cofounder of The Geneva School of Boerne and co-owner of the Urgent Care and Occupational Health Centers of Texas, PA.

Though a Christian since the age of seventeen, Dr. Fowler's battle with cardiac sarcoidosis was the catalyst to rediscovering his relationship with Christ—a union he knew and feared had been compromised for many years. He now acknowledges Christ every morning before letting his feet touch the floor. Dependence on his spiritual pacemaker never ceases.

A Note to Readers

*While I chronicled my **conversation**, I had no intention of writing a story, much less a book. It was an exercise in reflection and provided an avenue for me to witness God's presence in my life during a very wearisome time. Throughout my book's development over the past year and a half, I was given a refreshed view of my identity in Christ as seen through the lens of His Gospel. I am grateful for this opportunity and know I will never stop peering through these lenses again.*

The "success" of my book is not my concern, but my stewardship with any proceed is. From day one I committed to prayer that its content would reach the hearts of those it is intended. I have made a commitment to give fifty percent of the book's profits (if blessed as such) to organizations that I believe provide assistance, care and provision for those of any age who are in need, impoverished, or unable to care for themselves. During this past year, Cindy and I have identified four organizations meeting these requirements that have touched us personally.

Hill Country Daily Bread

Court Appointed Special Advocates (CASA) for Children

Empowered to Connect

Doctors Without Borders/Médecins Sans Frontières (MSF)

Access to the home web page of each organization has been posted on my book's website and Facebook page. If you would like to learn more about these organizations I invite you to research their sites.

CPSIA information can be obtained at www.ICGtesting.com
Printed in the USA
LVOW13s2156120614

389778LV00004B/6/P